Bless the world
with your talents.

Linda Lorincz

Aspirations for Success:
Blueprinting your future

By Linda J. Loving

INFINITY
PUBLISHING.COM

Copyright © 2009 by Linda J. Loving

ISBN 0-7414-5611-7

Editor: Lolita Cummings Carson

Illustrations: Linda J. Loving

Published by:

PUBLISHING.COM

1094 New DeHaven Street, Suite 100
West Conshohocken, PA 19428-2713
Info@buybooksontheweb.com
www.buybooksontheweb.com
Toll-free (877) BUY BOOK
Local Phone (610) 941-9999
Fax (610) 941-9959

Printed in the United States of America

Published October 2009

Acknowledgments

To Philip Jr., my wonderful husband of 18 years, a true friend, the lover of my heart, and love of my life. Thank you for encouraging me to follow my dreams. Thank you for being strong when I am weak. May God continue to bless you.

To my mother Dorothy Miller, the one who loves me unconditionally and prays for me with fervent prayers. I honor you, love you, and thank you for my upbringing.

Special thanks to my editor, Lolita Cummings Carson, APR. Lolita holds a Master's of Science Degree in Communications and more than 15 years as a university professor who specializes in professional writing. She has more than two decades of experience in public relations and owns her own public relations firm, Cummings Communications.

An additional thank you goes to my family and friends who kindly offered a listening ear and encouraging words.

Dedication

Many people were on my heart when I wrote this book. I dedicate this book to readers all over the world. May it inspire you to reach out and become all you have ever imagined. May it support and motivate you in your search for personal growth and life-long happiness. Today is the day you will find hope and strength to move forward toward a promising future -- the kind of future you dream of. May this inspirational reading and blueprinting bring you confidence and enthusiasm to plan your future.

Table of Contents

Introduction

Congratulations on your purchase of "Aspirations for Success, Blueprinting Your Future." To have an aspiration is to have a strong desire to achieve something noble. Many of us have aspirations, but don't quite know what to do with them. That is why I have laid out six basic principles in this book to help you create the blueprint of a plan for your future that can turn your strong desires into the attainment of your aspirations.

This book is both inspirational and educational. It is written with a wholehearted effort to inspire you to act on your aspirations -- not only to anticipate your future, but to draw a plan for your future. The inspirational part of this book is designed to share highlights from my life, filled with light humor at times and also to share some lessons I have learned from my life experiences. The educational part of this book will take you through a systematic process for making good and, in some cases, better decisions when planning your future. There are also assessments and practical principles that will motivate: successful thinking, goals planning, and the execution of a concise plan. This book is intended to motivate you to jumpstart your life plans. Why put off for tomorrow what you should do today? As I said before, you will be able to consider successful ways of thinking and reacting to life situations when it comes to your desire to achieve success.

<u>_Print Your Name_</u> this book was written just for you. I aspire to speak to your heart today because you have great potential. Through your potential you will do and become someone of great interpersonal strength, someone with an abundance of confidence, someone who will inspire all who cross your path. You could be the next famous author, the next rocket scientist, or even the next political leader. In this great time of life, you can do just about anything you intend to do. Do you also believe this? Have you begun to invest into that belief? Have you begun to use your potential? Do you even know your potential? Think about it! I hope so, because "Aspirations for Success, Blueprinting your future" is ready to help you advance to the next level in your life.

If you approach each chapter with an open mind, you will rediscover some things about yourself and possibly learn things you didn't realize before. If you have been wondering what has been holding you back from success, with a little effort, you are about to find out. Get ready to be inspired and to make some changes in the way you make choices for your future. This book will consistently remind you of the importance of how thoughtful planning is the key to pursuing your ultimate goals.

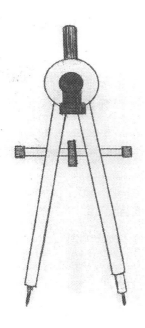

I was led to write this book when I suddenly realized how little time we really have to reach our goals, touch the lives of others, and to simply be happy. Life happens at a fast pace, but some people don't realize it until time has gone by, and then it's nearly too late. So now is the time to start planning.

Some parts of this book may sound spiritual. In fact, some of the principles in this book may indeed be used for spiritual application. I will take you on my own personal journey of hopes and desires to awaken your greatest hunger for success, which is indeed very spiritual to me. In fact, I believe all humans have a spiritual aspect to their lives. Without a doubt, the principles you will learn will benefit you in many ways.

"Aspirations for Success" is your opportunity to assess what you already have and, by blueprinting, make it even better. Why a blueprint? Blueprints lay out details, and details can be used for future plans of action. Once you have completed your details, you will be able to make informed decisions from a fresh perspective. Then you can determine for yourself whether you are bound for success or headed toward failure.

You may have taken notice of how blueprinting is significant in many aspects of life. Authors have written about blueprinting for weight loss and financial gain. Blueprints are also used in mechanical drawings by architects, and in many other ways. Imagine along with me what your life would be like if you blueprinted your pathway to a successful future and began to work your plan of action. A personal blueprint will allow you to see your life's journey on paper. It will allow you to see the things you can change, make better, and build upon. This will instill confidence that you are on the right path.

Chapter 1, "Who Are You?" focuses on the importance of knowing one's self. Who are you? Self can be our worst enemy. Think about your past, present and future. The object of this chapter is to begin a self-study. It inspires self-honesty and self-confidence when looking at the good and not so good things about your past and present in order to proceed toward a better future. You will take a short assessment and answer some simple questions about yourself, your family and friends, likes and dislikes, and so forth. There are no right or wrong answers to the assessment. I only ask that you be open and honest with yourself in order to get a good perception of who you are. It shouldn't take someone else to tell you who you are. You should know for yourself without hesitation.

Chapter 2, "Inner Being," is about your inner self. It is a look at the personal behaviors and characteristics that could possibly motivate you to move to the next level in your career, relationships, and life -- or could cause you to be held back from becoming successful. You will take a short assessment and answer some simple questions about your behavior. Again, there are no right or wrong answer keys to the assessment. I only ask that you be open and honest with yourself in order to get a good look at yourself and the full capability of your inner being. You may find that you could be better.

Chapter 3, "Outer Actions," will help you to understand just why you do the things you do, from choosing friendships to actions and reactions. You will begin to see the people who influence you the most for who they really are. You will be challenged and questioned about your relationships. Everything you do plays an important part in your future success. Believe it or not, other people also play an impor-tant role in your success. All of the exercises are created to give you food for thought, and to help create a virtual picture of how your outer actions are conveyed. Consequently, you will be able to make better choices for your future, choices that will bring forth a lifetime of rewards.

Chapter 4, "The Mentor," will invite you to choose mentors who inspire you to go beyond the norms of what you may think or what you may have been told in the past. In this chapter, you will see how to choose virtual mentors who are extremely successful. This chapter explains how you can choose mentors from any time and any walk of life. They can be famous mentors who you have never met and/or mentors from the past. Just choose an inspiring person to help you map your own pathway to a successful future.

I'd like to add that modeling mentors can help you avoid some of the pitfalls, bumps and bruises in life. Although people do make bad choices and bump their heads from time-to-time, (because that's how some people learn) who in the world would prefer to have an ugly lump on their forehead as opposed to some great advice and a pretty face? Furthermore, once you make a bad choice and put it into action, you have sealed the deal. Often, there is no turning back, and the decision could be devastating to you or someone you love.

Chapter 5, "Get in the Competition," and Chapter 6, "Building a Legacy," continue to empower you to reach your ultimate goals. In Chapter 5, you will be encouraged to get into the game. You should be "In the Competition" instead of outside of it, or worst yet, oblivious that there is even a competition going on. Last, but not least, Chapter 6 empowers you to create a legacy for yourself and the people in your life.

I encourage you to find a quiet place to read and concentrate. The signing of the Personal Blueprinting Agreement on the next page signifies your commitment to work your way through this book, and to give a whole-hearted effort toward understanding the basic principles and applying them to your life. Do this and you will go from surviving to excelling with your personal blueprint. Your life will start to change for the better. So without further adieu, thank you for joining me, and let's get started.

Personal Blueprinting Agreement

I acknowledge the receipt of this Personal Blue-printing Agreement. I understand and agree that I will give a whole-hearted effort toward understanding these basic principles and faithfully working through the exercises to enrich my life. I am committed to being open-minded when taking a look at my own actions and associations. This is a study of self. Furthermore, I agree to be committed to making a plan for my future, and I understand that my results depend on my honesty and commitment.

Signed: _____

Date: _____

Chapter 1
Who Are You?

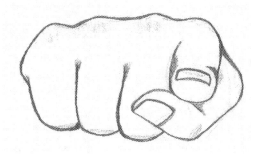

*W*e live in an age where a vast amount of information can be shared and obtained. In fact, there is information available on virtually any subject you want to learn about, including learning more about yourself. With the help of books and computers, you can read about everything from the lifestyles of the rich and famous, to the lifestyles of others in foreign countries. You can learn how to fly an airplane and how to speak a foreign language without the help of a personal instructor. It's amazing how much you can learn via the Internet alone to broaden your intellect. Many people spend lots of time learning about other people, places and things. And that's good because learning is vital to your survival in this world. For that reason, there is hardly an excuse for anyone who has access to knowledge to be without it today. However, it is interesting to know that many people will go to great extremes to learn about everything and everyone else – just not about themselves. If you ask them questions such as, "Who are you?" "What is your purpose?" and/or "What do you want to be in life?" most people will reply by saying, "I don't know." That is why this chapter is dedicated to helping you answer this very important question – "Who are you?" When you obtain *that* answer, the other answers will fall into place.

Principle 1: You must get to know yourself

Knowing yourself and being confident in who you are is an important aspect of self esteem.

Food for thought: *Knowing yourself creates a strong foundation to gain the confidence to become the person you are destined to be.*

When I was growing up, I didn't understand how important it was to know myself. However, as an adult, I realize that if I don't know myself, it's difficult to articulate to others just who I really am. I learned the hard way that faking it doesn't always work. The bottom line is that when I pretend to know myself or to be confident, in the end, I feel cheated and insecure. The solution is to become comfortable with self and all of its qualities and assets.

There are some people who grew up in a family environment knowing exactly who they were and what they wanted to become. Perhaps they were instilled with this knowledge at an early age and were encouraged to be confident in who they were and who they hoped to become. Those few may even take it for granted by thinking this is something everyone should know automatically, when, in fact, this revelation does not come instinctively. There are many people who don't know themselves, and the little that they do know, they think is insignificant. There are even some who seek out others to tell them who they are and what their future holds. You may have seen them standing in lines waiting for their future to be revealed by someone else.

Throughout this chapter, you will have the opportunity to begin your self-study and start a personal blueprint. It will allow you the opportunity to really think and meditate on various words and questions. Some of the areas of your life that you will have a chance to ponder include:

1. **Family, Friends, Associations**
2. **Self-Assessment**
3. **Ambition and Goals**
4. **Personal Traits**

These areas include outside links to who you are and will enable you to take a deeper look at the person you are now and the person you could become. I write, who "you could become," because many people are or have been hiding behind a shell that has covered their real personalities and, in many ways, it has caused them to not fully develop into the person they could become. I'm no spiritual teacher, but I know enough to know that our lives mean something. Not just mine, not just yours, but every one of us.

Getting to know yourself – a wise choice

According to the definition in *The Merriam –Webster Dictionary*, "to be wise is simply to have or to show good sense or judgment." Studying yourself is very wise. To know yourself, you must study yourself just as you would study a book. Consider my experience during the first job interview I ever had: The store owner asked me to talk about myself, my strengths, and my plans for the future. He wanted to know about the valuable skills I could offer and how I could benefit the company. It was a great question. The problem is that I wasn't prepared with an answer. My first thought was, "Is this a trick question?" I also thought that it was a little intense for a cashier/clerk position. However, in retrospect, I understand that the business owner simply wanted to know something about the type of person I was then and what I hoped to become in the future. He wanted to know if I had ever given any thought about my future. So many younger people haven't given enough thought about their future. This is typical, but it is not wise.

That was when I began to realize that I was lacking some very important information about myself. I also realized something very important and useful from that experience. There are some people who are well spoken and have the ability to interview very well. These people have thought about the path of life they want to walk. Some of these individuals possess the great skill of casual and formal conversation. They can easily articulate their worth, plans and skills. Sadly, at that time, I wasn't one of them.

Have you ever been asked to talk about yourself in a formal setting? How did it make you feel and what was your response? Did you run out of information after stating your name, where you work, and perhaps where you go to school -- or did you dig deeper and share information about your character, personality, skills, abilities or ambitions? You are so much more than a few brief words describing your exterior characteristics. You are much more than your attire, your vehicle, your home, or your job. You are who you are from the inside out. From birth until now you were pro-grammed to believe something, to feel something, to act and to react. Just who is the inner person that people see and meet everyday? Don't you want to know? Well, you *should* know and you should be able to put your values into words quickly, precisely and confidently.

We all have something unique about us that is potentially valuable information and that should be shared with others. We all have a mind, a body and a soul. Our minds are full of untapped creativity waiting to be explored, developed and unleashed. Our hearts and souls anticipate the satisfaction felt by touching and inspiring others in some positive way -- just because we are human, or perhaps because of our purpose.

If you are a person who likes to help others, then you could be a nurse, lawyer, doctor, social worker or a missionary. If you are a great communicator, you could be an anchor-person, a teacher, a television host, or a public speaker. Within you is potential to go where you have only dreamt of going and to do what you always wanted to do. As time moves on, the world changes, and so should you.

However, there are some things about you that will remain the same unless *you* decide to change. Everyday that you change and grow older, you should endeavor to become wiser by intentionally getting to know yourself as well as the world around you. You should expose yourself to new things and challenge yourself on higher levels. It is what I call having intentional and preconceived knowledge about you and who you want to become, stored up and waiting to be released. In other words, don't just get older -- get better, stronger, wiser, and be more confident.

Life is short, so start planning your future now.

My elderly mother summed it up perfectly when she said, "LIFE IS SHORT. I don't know where the time went." I have heard many people use the phrase, "LIFE IS SHORT." Some of them were younger than I am. However, it really caught my attention when my mother said it. Her statement rings true for us all. Many younger people view the elderly as old because they have lived lives longer than ours. However, many of them may believe their lives have gone by too quickly. They have learned just how big and rich this world is, and they are just starting to have fun. And that should be a lesson to us all.

Life is so precious and should be both valued and nurtured. Everything about your present will in someway affect your future, and the future of someone who you say you love. As I've heard some people say, "what goes in will come out," or maybe that's "what goes up will come down." However, extend the effort to nourishing yourself internally and externally, and value will be added to your life. It's as simple as that. Waiting without putting forth action only depletes your time. Life is now, and while you are alive, (and if you are reading this book, you are alive) you should live your life in abundance. Ask yourself, "What am I waiting for?" After all, remember that time is not waiting for you, so use your time wisely.

So who are you? First start by considering who you think you are. What words do you use to describe yourself?

Name three positive attributes that distinguish you from your friends and relatives.

1. _____

2. _____

3. _____

Name three attributes that you are known by, but you would like to improve.

1. _____

2. _____

3. _____

Is there something specific about the way you talk, think or interact with others that make you stand out from others? Do they make you stand out positively or negatively? When you know who you are, you will have a clear view of who you want to become. You will have a view of what and where you can contribute your value as a human being. That is what living is about.

What's the purpose?

Are you one to believe that you do not have a purpose in life? If so, here is my question to you: "Why in the world do you believe you have been singled out to not have a purpose in life?" Of course you have purpose. Don't be silly. Don't sell yourself for cheap; everyone has a purpose. What makes you less worthy of purpose than anyone else? The answer is, ABSOLUTELY NOTHING! We all have a purpose, but it's up to you to find yours. You must find your purpose and start living it to the fullest. To do this, you must have a good understanding of who you really are. Do you want positive things to happen in your life? Are you positive? Now, throughout this book continue to ask yourself the question, "Who am I?" You will see that asking and answering this question will help determine what you have the potential to become. However, you must be ready to answer honestly. You know that you are a product of your parents and your culture. That's easy. Dig deeper; find out what is truly inside. Only then will you find who you really are. All of the other things about you are exterior characteristics that can change or remain.

The potential is already within you.

When I was a young girl, I loved playing in the basement at home. One of the things I loved most was pretending to preach a sermon. I remember preaching to my younger sister and brother as we played pretend church. Sometimes I also preached to my imaginary audience as I played alone. However, as I reminisce, I can see how those incidents of playtime were very significant in my childhood. Even though it was pretend, I still remember feeling a level of excitement about pretending. It was something I enjoyed doing. I loved the idea of motivating and inspiring others, even though no one was really listening. That's who I was. Back then I had a lot to share on my imaginary platform. Then I grew up.

I am sharing this portion of my childhood story, not because I think I missed my calling to be a minister or a spiritual leader, although I do believe that inspiring spiritually and motivating others to physical action is very much a part of my purpose. No, I'm sharing this information because I believe it is important to pay attention to childhood aspirations. It is equally important to encourage the potential within children. Keep in mind that children have purpose too. In fact, I believe that purpose has been within us all for a very long time. That greatness that children have on the inside may seem small and insignificant to an untrained eye, but it may one day grow up to touch many lives. However, it will never touch anyone if it remains dormant inside or if it loses its ambition.

Recognize your potential and start using it.

As I said before, then I grew up. Unfortunately, as idle time goes by, bad habits tend to form. For a while I developed a bad habit called laziness, which zaps energy and ambition. If you want to go nowhere fast, then laziness is the avenue to take. The worst thing about having a lazy mindset is that you lose all sense of time. You actually can't even see it coming until one day you wake up with nothing to show for your life. Those of us who are older know very well that when it comes to time, we find that the old saying is true -- time truly is of the essence.

After useless efforts and trying to take the easy way out, fortunately, for me, I began to realize that I was going nowhere fast. I didn't have to become a navigator to figure out that rocky road. A part of my stagnation came from my not knowing what I wanted to do with my life. This may sound familiar to you. I attribute it to not having a good understanding of why planning for the future is so important when a person is young. Many young people are so wrapped up in the things going on in their present that they can't see the relevance of thinking about tomorrow. Most times they get blinded by such things as having a significant other, or having "in-the-moment fun" that can result in a lifetime of misery or burden. These individuals have great potential, but, unfortunately, they have little direction. Blueprinting enables you to set up a plan that gives direction.

For this reason, I want to create a virtual picture in your mind, with the help of stories, self assessments and charts. With this virtual picture, hopefully, you will begin to see the negatives that can come from an unplanned life and the positive things that can arise from a well planned life. Developing a plan creates direction. Direction leads to focus, endurance, and encourages a steady building of goals. The development stage alone will allow you the opportunity to add value to your plan. Don't let a lack of planning cause you to become stagnant. Make plans, review your plans often, and keep building. You are bound to succeed.

You've got potential!

You have potential. Everyone does, and it is a funny thing, although I'm not laughing anymore. However, it is funny and kind of strange at the same time. It can remain dormant within you until you decide to develop it into something great. But you have to believe in yourself and be willing to take a chance on that belief. It's up to you to develop and use your potential to find your purpose.

Food for thought: If you become stagnant in your personal growth, revisit the reasons you started your journey to success in the first place and regain your passion to succeed.

People want to succeed for different reasons. The reason could be hidden from them because of missing information. Studying yourself causes you to dig deep to find the real reason. Personally, my missing information dealt with my need to get to know myself in order to have confidence in my potential.

Working in the area of human resources has helped to restore my childhood aspirations. It has taught me that I have a passion and a purpose to share insightful information that can enhance the lives of others. Getting to know yourself and exploring your potential will enable you to find your purpose. Knowing yourself is a liberating experience. It will help you to avoid making excuses about why things are not going well in your life and get down to the business of fixing it. You will actually begin to figure out what to do about it, and that will lead to living a more satisfying life.

Recognize your need to change or improve for times sake.

Change is something that happens every day of our lives. You change, I change, the whole world changes. It is up to each and every one of us to keep up with our need for change and improvement. It is also up to us to implement improvements in our lives and decide not to settle for less than the very best. I encourage you to be the best you can be as you complete this blueprint for your future.

You may find that improvements need to occur in a specific area of your life or in several areas. In this section, as you focus on your need to improve, also begin to identify the reasons that you think you may need to improve. Only you can truly observe and identify what improvements are needed. As you focus, don't think of these areas in a negative manner. Think of these as areas for potential growth, as opportunities. Begin by understanding why things are like they are currently, and what occurrences have brought you to this place in life.

For example: People who are only certified to be medical assistants are not qualified to work in the capacity of a registered nurse. However, they have the potential to grow into the nursing field if they pursue academics and training. When you become informed about your potential growth areas, hopefully, it will motivate you to make the choice to start growing. The process of changing and improving is not always easy and, as an individual, you can't possibly do it all at once. However, over time, your improvements will take form.

Recognizing my need for change was not a case of too much information; it was a case of information I didn't have. Incidentally, lack of information is one common reason why people fail. Many things can cause people to lack information. My solution was that I needed to understand and find what I was missing in order to go on to the next step. A personal struggle I had was learning how to take and use constructive and non-constructive criticism to my benefit. It was a long and painful process; however, it was one that was needed in my life before I could move toward my goal of leadership. More than likely, it is the same for you.

Change! Who? Me?

What if you could find your missing link, your missing piece to the puzzle of success? What do you think it would be? What would enable you to actually move to the next level in your life? Knowing the answer to those questions could clearly help you to connect the dots of your life, enabling you to hit the target of success. This is not rocket science. The simple fact is that if you don't know that something is wrong, you won't try to fix it. In other words, if you have a goal in mind, but you keep missing the pieces that are important to your puzzle of success, you'll want – and need -- to see the full picture.

You can always tell for yourself when you are missing pieces. Just ask yourself, what's next for me? If you can't answer that with even a ballpark estimate, then something is missing. Let me ask you a few questions. Have you settled for less? Is being the mediocre store clerk your ultimate goal, or do you have potential to become the manager or owner? How about being the careless service provider? Is that your only future endeavor, or do you yearn to step up to the plate because of your life, reputation, and integrity?

To find the missing pieces, just measure your current circumstances against a long-term plan to see if they measure up. Do you even have a long-term plan? If so, what is it? Jot it down here. _____. I'm not referring to a thought. I'm talking about a real, viable, and documented plan, a blueprint. If you have some ideas, write them down.

You need a long-term plan and the ability to break that plan down into short-term plans. This will become your personal blueprint. It will help you to remember what you need to do next and to be diligent about meeting goals and setting new ones.

> *All our dreams can come true, if we have the courage to pursue them.*
> *Walt Disney*

Still can't tell? One way to see if you need a plan is to take a look at your situation, finances, need for more education, lifestyle, and relationships. Those things tend to cast a reflection on our life's value. You can find the answer by measuring them for lack of progress and potential growth. Do they meet a standard that is satisfactory to you? After you measure them, start making plans to improve in these areas.

Remember that you can only do what you know how to do. Furthermore, you will only be called on to do what you are capable of doing. You can't be a certified practitioner without the certification and training. Neither can you be a pilot if you don't know how to fly an airplane. That is precisely why you should take a closer look at the areas of your life that you want to expand.

My whole point is to continually encourage and motivate you to move forward toward your future goals. I know some people may choose to find out the hard way by wasting precious time, but don't let that happen to you. To put it plainly, you will not be satisfied with an unplanned and unfinished life when it is all said and done. There are many people who have fallen into this category. You may have noticed them as you've passed by. You may have even pitied them. But if you learn from their mistakes, there is a good chance that you will not fall into the same category because of bad choices. You have an opportunity to make better choices. We will pinpoint more areas in the chapters to come.

Life's Turning Points

The lists below contain personal enhancements, life detours, and harmful actions that can cause major change in a person's future plans. Use this list to select turning points that you choose to allow to impact your future. The blank lines below each list are provided for you to write in other life turning points that you may think of.

Personal Enhancement
- ☐ Education/Skills
- ☐ Employment
- ☐ Sports
- ☐ Mentor/Tutor
- ☐ Memberships
- ☐ Organization/Association
- ☐ Career
- ☐ Etiquette
- ☐ College
- ☐ Hobby
- ☐ Volunteerism
- ☐ Finances

_____

_____

_____

Personal Detour
- ☐ Dropout
- ☐ Large Purchases
- ☐ Friendship
- ☐ Laziness
- ☐ Fear
- ☐ Marriage
- ☐ Relationship

_____

_____

_____

Harmful Action
- ☐ Dropout
- ☐ Violence
- ☐ Impurity
- ☐ Depression
- ☐ STD
- ☐ Drugs
- ☐ Laziness
- ☐ Stubbornness
- ☐ Alcohol
- ☐ Imprisonment
- ☐ High Risk Activity

_____

_____

_____

What will it take to encourage you to take a stand for the good of your future? What will it take to encourage you to really start digging through your life and make healthy changes for enhancement? Begin by recognizing and acknowledging your potential and be true to yourself -- the real you. You are stronger, smarter, greater, and more talented than you have yet revealed. You have the right to choose the best options for your future.

Blueprint 1

Family, Friends and Associations

Name	
Nickname(s):	**Education Level:**
Father's Name:	Mother's Name:
Education Level:	Education Level:
Father's Father:	Mother's Father:
Education Level:	Education Level:
Father's Mother:	Mother's Mother:
Education Level:	Education Level:
Sister(s):	
Education Level:	
Brother(s):	
Education Level:	
Special Friend(s):	
Education Level:	
Why is this your special friend? What is special about him/her?	
Best Friend(s):	
Education Level:	
How are you compatible with your best friends?	

Blueprint 1

Family, Friends ad Associations

Name:

Favorite Color(s):
Least favorite color(s):
Favorite Food(s):
Least favorite food(s):
Favorite Book(s):
Least favorite book(s):
Favorite Thing(s):
Least favorite thing(s):
Favorite Season of Year:
Least favorite season(s):
Favorite Conversational Subject:
Least favorite conversation:
Favorite Car(s):
Least favorite car(s):
Favorite Drink(s):
Least favorite drink(s):

Blueprint 1

Self Assessment

Describe something you love about yourself.
What is your best asset?
Describe your personality.
Describe something that you don't like about yourself and would like to improve.
How can you go about making the improvement?
Where do you see yourself in five years?
What are some of the positive things you see about life and your future?
If you could have any lifestyle you wanted, how would you live?
What kind of person do you want to be?

Blueprint 1

Ambitions and Goals

Career Choices:

Highest Educational Goal:

What are your talent(s)?

How can you use them to further your success?

What are your activities?

How can you use them to further your success?

If you could have any career in the world, what would it be?

When it comes to your future, what do you look forward to? Why?

When it comes to your future, what are you afraid of? Why?

Blueprint 1

Personal Traits

Categories	1	2	3	4	5
Interpersonal Skills	I have none.	I have some but they are rusty.	I do well -- better than most.	I have good skills.	Overly interpersonal. I talk too much.
Communication Skills	Not very good	Lots of slang	I do OK -- better than most.	I have good skills.	Well spoken
Body Language	Too stiff	A little sluggish	Better than most	I have good body language.	Very aware of the right way to carry myself
Appearance: Attire/Hair	Need grooming or over dressed	Under dressed	Better than most	Neat & Appropriate	Well groomed & stylish
Ethics	Immoral/ Evil	I do well some times.	Better than most	Good. -- I try to do the right thing.	Outstanding and trustworthy

If you experience low numbers on the assessments, I encourage you to look forward to pushing yourself a little harder during the next chapters. You can always improve your score. If we were all honest, we would all admit that we could use some improvement.

Principle 1

You must get to know yourself.

✓ Get to know yourself by studying yourself.

✓ Life is short, so start planning your future now.

✓ You have the potential already within.

✓ Recognize your potential and start using it.

✓ Recognize your need to change or improve.

✓ Nurture your talents and greatness.

Blueprint Notes 1

What area of your life would you like to learn more about?

_____

_____

_____

_____

_____

_____

_____

_____

Celebrate Chapter 1

Celebrate who you are! What are you going to do for yourself to celebrate completing chapter 1? Don't neglect to celebrate, and be sure to document it below.

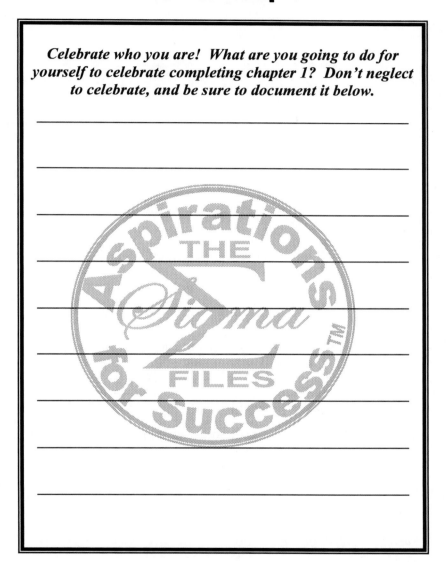

Chapter 2

Inner Being

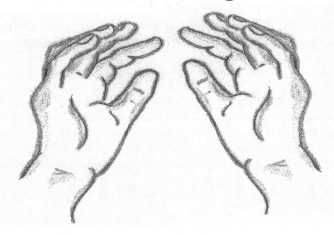

*M*any people spend their lives waiting for something good to happen to them instead of making good happen. Both young and old alike are waiting. Young women are waiting for a knight in shining armor, and young men are waiting for some big deal to unfold. Older women are waiting to marry some divorced or widowed man, and the older men are still waiting to hit the lottery. In fact, it seems that people are wasting time waiting while time swiftly passes them by. Why is this? As I mentioned in chapter 1, it's simply because of dormant potential. Potential can cause you to take chances in life and make experiences, or it can remain dormant. Unfortunately, it can eventually turn into laziness. So, if you have been waiting for your potential to kick in, or you are waiting for the old potential bug to bite you, Uh! Knock! Knock! Here it is! Again, potential is a funny thing. If applied, it can become great, genius and even profound; however, if it is not applied, it will simply remain internalized potential.

Principle 2: Plan for the future

Unfortunately, one of the greatest errors committed in a person's young life is the wasting of time. The assuming aspect about wasting time is that "time is always on your side." That seems to be the message that causes a lot of people to procrastinate in the first place. Let's take a look at a commonly noticed after-effect of wasting time. Many children waste time in school in the early years of their lives. They do not strengthen the foundational work that ensures them an opportunity to build a strong academic future. Therefore, by the time children get to middle school, they have formed so many bad habits (most times unbeknownst to them), that it's hard for them to escape the coming academic failures.

Why is this? Whose fault is it? Well, it is everyone's fault. You may ask, if it is the fault of the educational system, the parents, or the young people? Yes! On all counts, yes! The fact is that everyone must do the job they have been assigned to in order for the educational system to work most effectively.

- Teachers must be qualified to teach and identify problems that arise with students. They must also be willing to address the problems they find concerning the students' ability to learn the foundational curriculum. When the foundational understanding of students is not strong, it's difficult for them to keep up with the more advanced work. In this case, some students never rebound from early failures. The fact is that some of these students don't receive the help they need before being passed to the next grade level. Although some of these students can't read or write, it doesn't necessarily imply they can't learn. It simply means they are moving through the cracks of the educational system without having these vital problems addressed. I'm sure this is not a new finding—we have all seen students who are not ready to pass to the next grade, but they do so anyway. If no child is to be left behind, these issues must be addressed as early as possible.

- Parents must sacrifice time and get involved with their children's education. When children can't read, write and do math in the early years of their life, more than likely, they will continue to form bad habits unless these issues are addressed. Who is better to address this problem than their parents, who can clearly see the children in their everyday activity? It is the parents who see their children outside playing when they should be studying. Their bad habits will eventually catch up with them and become a hinder to their success in adulthood. Some parents form a negative attitude when being told their children can't read or write -- or that they have low skills. Instead, parents should appreciate the early warnings. This type of information should serve as a wake up call for help. Most of the time parents already know their children need additional help; however, a lot of parents haven't stopped going about their own lives long enough to assess their children's needs.

- Parents should stop and listen to see if their children can read before it gets out of hand -- that's a parent's job. Parents should be willing to do what's right for their children so they can take full advantage of all opportunities. Remember, children love to play. That's what they do. It is the parent's job to help them to distinguish what they can and can not play with. Education is something they should not be allowed to play with, and it should be taken seriously.

For example, a good caring parent wouldn't let their children play with a mountain lion; likewise, a caring parent shouldn't let their children play with their education. Again, children love to play. It is up to parents to help them distinguish when and when not to play, and to understand how costly it is to their future.

- To the younger people who are trying to get it together, just think about this. If you decide to be the class clown throughout your school years, in the years to come, the joke will surely turn on you. There may be a few classmates laughing at you. They may even appear to agree with you, by saying phrases like, "You're so crazy." But don't let this fool you. In the end, there will be no one laughing with you and, unfortunately, there will be no one who can help you. So be wise and do the right thing. When you become an adult, you won't want to hear people say, "You're so crazy." Making the extra effort now to ensure a stable future may be a little hard, but taking on the responsibility to grow your life and value is well worth it. You are smart enough to figure that out. It may be tedious, but you have the time right now. Enjoy making wise choices for your life.

Blame Game

If people will just pause for just a minute, stop blaming everyone else for their personal failures, and turn the mirror to their own faces, every individual will actually see the person who can find a solution to make their life better. Just like the tiny ants you have noticed on the pavement, working away in the hot summer months to store up food for the coming winter, every single person should be working to secure their future and well-being. While you are young, you should not only take time to enjoy life, but also to plan for your future, and execute your plan. As you may have heard many others say, "if you fail to plan, you are really planning to fail."

At the end of Chapter 2, you will begin making life plans with the help of some simple exercises. You will have the opportunity to:

Pinpoint your:

a. Strengths: the quality of being strong; toughness
How do you handle life's pressure?

_____
_____

Name three of your personal strengths:

_____
_____

Name three of your professional strengths:

_____

_____

b. Weaknesses: lacking strength; feeble

Name three of your personal weaknesses:

_____

_____

Name three of your professional weaknesses:

_____

_____

Food for thought: *If you allow yourself to become lazy when you are young, you take the chance of letting your best years slip through your fingers without having the opportunity to invest in valuable input.*

There was a time when I wasted time. However, at some point, I began to realize that my life was passing me by, and I didn't have anything to show for it. The time seemed to have evaporated overnight, although I knew it really hadn't. However, I now understand just how swiftly time can pass. Once upon a time you and I were small children, and now just look at us – all grown up. Time goes by fast, and it will continue to do so. Think about this. If a person sleeps eight hours a day and works eight hours a day, there are only eight hours left in a single day to plan, prepare and enjoy life.

How will you spend your eight hours, and what will you do to get the most out of your precious time?

What do you consider to be a waste of time? The answer is basically the same for us all. Even when we are sleeping, the clock steadily ticks away. One day you could be roaming along in your youth wasting time, bobbing your head, and popping your fingers to the beat, and miss the whole point of being young in the first place. Youth is where you should start making preparations for the rest of your life. It's where you are taught values, where you experience love, and where you learn to respect. So when you are older, you can teach, be loved, and respect others.

You may have the solution to a problem that exists in your community, your church, or in your school. It could be a solution to help people in your neighborhood or around the world. How cool would that be?

Who? YOU! Life planning is for everyone.

Viewing the world as it is today, what kind of future do you want for yourself and your family? If ever there was a time to commit to a cause that can improve your future, it is now. Neighborhoods and communities are full of people who haven't given any care and concern for their future welfare or their family's future. There are signs before their very eyes, such as rising unemployment due to outsourcing, bankruptcies, the increasing need for skilled workers in largely unskilled populations, and other economic indicators, yet this still hasn't prompted people to get moving toward a solution. Part of the problem is that when people accept low standards out of life, don't educate themselves, and are satisfied with living in sub-standard conditions, it is very possible that their families will follow their lead. When you take a realistic look at your personal finances, your prospects for employment or a career, and your situation as a whole, how secure do you feel about your present lifestyle and your future welfare?

☐ **Not secure at all. I need a plan.**

☐ **I feel okay, but I still need a plan.**

☐ **I feel very secure, but a good plan is always a great.**

There are some people who will still choose to waste their lives or put forth very little effort into securing a good future. What would cause them to waste so much precious time? What causes people to destroy their own communities where they live with their families, their parents, grandparents, and where their children play and go to school? I am sure there are a variety of reasons. Some of them we have no control over. It is true that we may not be able to save the world, but we can save ourselves and help some of our family members. The ugly and vicious cycle created from having a purposeless life or having little to no self worth has to stop with someone. Why not make it stop with you and in your generation?

Many people live in communities that have been destroyed by other people because of drugs and petty and violent crimes. This devastates entire neighborhoods and communities at a rate that ignorance can't comprehend. It shuts down businesses and destroys many people's lives and livelihood. In these communities, jobs are lost and students are dropping out of schools at an increasingly high rate. Why is this? Is it because they have no hope or ambition, or maybe they have never been encouraged to do much of anything else. As for the student dropouts, perhaps they have fallen behind in their academics. Is it because they can't comprehend the material? This is a huge problem. Not only can it destroy a young person's life, but the devastation can have a rippling effect on entire families.

There is absolutely no reason for people to drop out of school just because they have gotten behind or feel like they are not at the level of their classmates. Education is all about helping people get caught up to speed. For example, I may not be able to process numbers like Einstein, but I have my very own purpose. Dropping out is not the answer. It can result in dormant potential and negative energy. Just because you can't save the world doesn't mean you can't do your part to improve it. Now, you may ask the question: "Am I my brother's keeper?" Today, I say YES!! You are your brother's keeper, as well as your mother's, father's, sister's, cousin's, and neighbor's. We all have a responsibility to help one another.

Exactly how are you planning to safeguard yourself and your family? It is important to think about these things. There are so many things that can negatively affect your family. In fact, have you ever thought about how a negative environment will impact your future? If not, now is the time to do so.

In chapter 1 you started a study of yourself as an individual. Here in chapter 2 you are beginning to broaden your exploration and answer questions like, "what are your strengths and weaknesses?" and "what are your circumstances?" and "how do your circumstances and actions affect others?" You will also learn to make better choices for your future and to use moderation in making those choices. Greatness is already within you. It is waiting for you to make something good happen in your life and possibly the lives of others.

Where? Implement improvements to access new opportunities

Making simple lifestyle improvements can help you to access new opportunities. As you build your blueprint, begin to identify the changes you may need to make in order to reach new levels of your goal. Never be afraid to try new things that might challenge you personally. Keep in mind that life is full of challenges. You can't avoid them, but you can readjust and keep going.

This process of creating a personal blueprint is not only for adults; it is for young people and children as well. In fact, I recommend including children into this process. You will need to purchase a book especially for them, seeing that you have already begun to use this one for your personal documentation. It is important that your children know for certain that they also need a plan in place for their future. They will not *always* be children, and it is unfair to send them out in this cold world unprepared. So, as you build your plan for life, help them to build theirs. Help them to begin to identify the constant changes they will have to make to attain success. It is important for them to visualize a future as well.

Things have certainly changed from how it used to be when I was younger. Children could run freely in their neighborhoods and experience life. Parents were not afraid to let their children play outside, ride their bikes, meet new friends, and be creative. When I was 11 years old, my younger sister and I would play outside everyday in the front yard in our neighborhood. We were free to create childhood games, songs and dances. I remember one song and dance we made up right on our front porch was called, "Hello, I like to be with you." You see, in those days, we could play on our front porch, in the backyard, and even up the street without mom being worried that something bad would happen to us. Those were the good old days. I'm not asking for those days to return, only that people begin to understand what happens when you take away children's freedom and creativity. Neighborhoods dry up -- and hope diminishes.

So what happened? Today that same neighborhood has faced some devastation. On that very street, many houses that have not yet been torn down or boarded up are either vacant or in disrepair. The surrounding area is now infested with crime, drugs, and people with too much time on their hands. When I was growing up, people had more respect for themselves and their properties. They also had a higher regard for one another and needed not be afraid of one other. People took care of themselves, their families, their homes, and their properties. They taught their children to have a good outlook on life. However, looking back, I can almost see where some things began to go wrong. In some families there was a lack of information and resources. Little did people know, the pot was about to boil over, and the spill was not going to be pretty. Greed and selfishness crept into the hearts of people and turned some of them away from doing the right thing. This kind of action not only affects one's self, but families, friends, and others. In this case, the result was the devastation of people's lives and families.

Not everyone was bad, however. There were lots of people who were just trying to get a job and make ends meet for their families. But, there were also others, who, for one reason or another, didn't have ambitions to set goals for their lives. It's important to note that time didn't wait for them, and it won't wait for you either. I have a very vivid memory of sitting in my eighth grade classroom, writing a story about what I wanted life to be like when I graduated from high school. At times, I had to go to that stored memory in order to keep my dream alive, until I started blueprinting.

How? Begin to create a blueprint for your life and future.

If you ask any event planner, financial manager, or health advisor, they will all tell you that making plans and pursuing goals is a good thing to do in any situation. Falling on hard times, whether economic or personal, is not an excuse for not making plans. Although, I do have sympathy for people who have had hard times in life, because, I myself have had many hard times too, we all have to use our lessons learned as our own inspiration. However, what better time is there than right now to start with a clean slate. Forget about past procrastinations -- it's now time to move forward. There comes a time when you have to move on in order to see better days. It is time to take back what was lost by planning forward and by implementing change in order to capitalize on new opportunities. When you fail to put a plan in place for your life, you leave yourself open for failure. Many of us have heard the saying "move it or lose it." Well, you can use this same saying about your time.

Plans don't always seem to work out and sometimes circumstances change, but having a plan is far better than not having one. It doesn't matter if you are young or old, it's not too late to make a plan. In fact, make two or three plans. You know, A, B, and C. The more security you have for a successful future, the better.

Name three goals you want to attain.			
	A	**B**	**C**
GOAL			

Table 1: Goals

When I realized I needed a plan, I was already in my thirties. There was no time to wait for something good to happen to me. I started making what I call a blueprint of my future. By doing this, I soon found out that planning works.

It makes good sense to make good plans if you are planning on building a good life. A blueprint should include such things as professional and educational ambitions, personal goals, and financial goals. Blueprinting is a tool that allows you the ability to see your plans in action and to focus your attention where it is needed.

There are some people who automatically know what they want to do in life, while others tend to need a little help in the area of planning. If you are planning to increase your education, find someone who is qualified to help you. Counselors and advisors are there to take the pressure off of you, so that your educational experience goes as smoothly as possible. However, if your plans are non-educational, blueprinting will work for you as well. Perhaps you own a business and would like to grow it or your finances. You can use these exercises to blueprint your way to success in your field of choice.

What? Enjoying life now, but thinking ahead.

There are a lot of people with too much time on their hands. Idle time is not productive. I am not talking about the time that we all need to take a rest, reflect, enjoy life, or vacation. I am simply talking about wasted time doing things that will detract from your personal or professional growth. It adds up and eventually causes years to catch up.

In fact, idle time can lead to trouble for most people. Someone once said that idle time is the enemy's playground. In this context it means that idle time can easily be filled with non-productive and unlawful activity.

So what do you really want out of life? How long do you have to get to where you want to be in life? Do you have 20 years or 30 years to reach your goals? I asked this very important question to get you thinking about the subject of planning. Think about a time frame. Then write down the number of years it will take you to reach your goals. Add that number to your current age and you will know if you have sufficient time for planning. For example, if you are 20 years old and decide that in 20 years you want to have a certain lifestyle, you better start planning now. Don't let the accumulation of bad behavior and habits ruin your opportunity to have the lifestyle you want. A lot can happen in your life during the interim of 20 years. So be wise, plan, and pace yourself. You want to be sure to have a plan in action while you're enjoying life along the way.

Perhaps your goal is to become a lawyer, a scientist, a teacher, or a doctor; success in these careers won't happen over night. It takes planning, good health, patience and endurance. We should all have a dream become reality in our lifetime. All it takes is a plan. Think about it as we approach the next set of assessments. Your plan could actually be one that will inspire others.

Positive Events & Occurrence	Positive Events	Positive Events	Positive Events	Positive Events	Positive Events
START HERE → *Accomplishments*	Age: _____ Year: _____ Goal:	Age: _____ Year: _____ Goal:	Age: _____ Year: _____ Goal:	Age: _____ Year: _____ Goal:	Age: _____ Year: _____ Goal:
Negative Events & Occurrences	Negative Events	Negative Events	Negative Events	Negative Events	Negative Events

Positive Events	Positive Events	Positive Events	Positive Events	Positive Events	Positive Events
Age: _____ Year: _____ Goal:	Age: _____ Year: _____ Goal:	Age: _____ Year: _____ Goal:	Age: _____ Year: _____ Goal:	Age: _____ Year: _____ Goal:	Age: _____ Year: _____ Goal:
Negative Events	Negative Events	Negative Events	Negative Events	Negative Events	Negative Events

Table 2a: Long Term Planning 1   This chart is to be used to document yearly goals, events and occurrences (for example: a major move, a bad relationship, a change of plans, etc.) that happened along the way.

LONG TERM PLANNING										
—	**Goals**									
20	Final goal stage									
19										
18										
17										
16										
15										
14										
13										
12										
11										
10										
9										
8										
7										
6										
5										
4										
3										
2										
1	Beginning goal stage									
	Age									
	Year		20_	20_	20_	20_	20_	20_	20_	
			Age and Year goals are completed							

GOAL STAGES (left vertical label)

Mark an "X" in the box once you have completed a goal stage. (center vertical label)

Table 2b: Long Term Planning 2

Use this chart to lay out your long term planning. Start at Stage 1 and plan through Stage 20. For each goal accomplished, document your age and place an X in the box to signify the completion of the goal.

When? Now! Because time waits for no one

Timing is a very important factor in the ability to pursue goals. You must agree that it could be much easier and smarter to pursue certain goals while you are younger. Nevertheless, any time you set out to pursue goals, you will find that timing is a factor. In chapter 1, you learned that who you are reveals a variety of perspectives to knowing yourself. Defining who you are from your perspective, your family, friends, associations, and others gives you the confidence that you need to make better choices for your future. Planning your future gives you a clear sense of direction. If you are committed to planning, from this point on, you will find that it is all about commitment, patience, endurance, and, of course, timing.

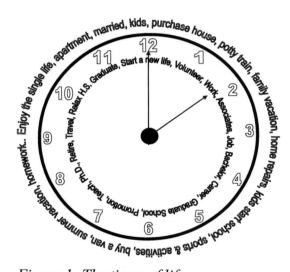

Figure 1: The times of life

Commitment is the virtuous part to pursuing a goal. This is especially true when it comes to everyday priorities such as working a full-time job, taking care of a family, or other everyday tasks. Commitments consume a lot of time. This makes it hard to commit to other goals and desires. However, just like normal priorities in life, we must place the life goals that will eventually sustain our life priorities at an equally important level. Considering that, the road to success can be long and tedious. However, realistically, the time will pass whether you commit to your goals or not. So the question is -- what are you doing with your time?

Get Moving

Maybe you're at a stand still in life. Are you thinking about how you can attain your goals faster? Do you have a goal in mind, but still wonder if this goal is also your purpose? When I hear people speak of finding their purpose, they tend to intellectualize the conversation. It's as if they think their purpose is so deeply buried and so mysterious that it would take an archeologist to dig it up and a fortune teller to read it. Yes, finding purpose is very important, but it's not rocket science. The creator of the world did not hide your purpose under a rock. To find your purpose, you must first know who you are. This was the lesson in chapter 1. By now you should not only be familiar with who you are, but very confident about it. Let's keep moving forward.

Why? Learning from others' mistakes

Many of my memories are embedded in the pages of this book. However, as I look back on my life, I've realized something very significant that's worth mentioning. Childhood aspirations without the proper guidance can lead to lost time. When I was growing up, my dream was to become someone who inspires others and to be a world-class opera performer. In my bedroom, I would sing the songs of my idols, Leontyne Price, Jesse Norman, and Barbara Streisand. I would sing their songs over and over again, committing them to my memory, paying special attention to the clarity of their vocals, their concise pronunciation, and the way the sound flowed through their vocal instruments. Back then I knew every crescendo and decrescendo, and every soft and loud note. When I was in jr. high school, I was exposed to the brilliantly composed music written by late great composers of the 17th, 18th, and 19th centuries. This made a huge impact on my young life. However, after my teenage years, my dreams seemed to have gotten lost for a long time due to a lack of preparation. That's why it's important to have a support system in place for your children and for yourself. As an adult, you can still learn to love the things you once loved, and do the things you once did.

Preparation means everything when it comes to realizing dreams and obtaining goals. If you prepare for something you want, more than likely you will have it. For example, when someone prepares for a job interview, it usually goes well. When someone saves money for a future purchase, at the right time, they buy the product. One reason people come up short is that they are unprepared.

Getting into the habit of being unprepared is a bad habit that is both noticeable and unattractive. Eventually, the accumulation of these bad habits and behaviors will not contribute to the realization of goals. On the other hand, the aspirations of our youth, once cultivated and developed, can be realized in a great way.

So, let me reiterate once again. A way to ensure the proper development of your aspirations is to study who you are and move in the right direction. Make sure to let others around you know your goals and future aspirations. By doing this you will be speaking your future into existence and you will also be involving others to help keep you accountable for your goals. Secondly, write your goals down as a reminder of what you need and want to do. It's okay if your goals change as you get older; just update them and keep going. Then begin to set your plans into action.

What? Changing learned behavior

I am not a psychologist; however, I would like to approach the subject of behavior from a human resources perspective. Almost everyday I meet people who are applying for jobs and pursuing careers. Many of the entry level candidates are unprepared for the interview process, not to mention the job. More and more often, I see people who possess lousy attitudes and express unhealthy behavior patterns that do not meet the standards of a safe and healthy work environment. Many times it causes them to be over looked for more suitable candidates.

Some behaviors are a product of our upbringing and have been a part of us since birth. The definition of a *learned behavior* is a "behavior pattern that a person has observed and taken on because they have found it to be beneficial to them in some way." Usually there are motivating factors behind behaviors and conditions that depend on stimuli that are triggered by personal intent. Although some learned behaviors and habits are hard to break, that is not to say that every behavior cannot be changed. Most can.

Many authors have researched and written on this very subject. One way in particular to change learned behaviors and bad habits is by learning. People learn such things as etiquette and proper behavior to fit in socially. Etiquette is taught to prepare students for various interactions. This is done because the ways people react in social situations can be both appropriate and inappropriate, depending on the setting. Knowing how to act and react in social situations is not always common sense. Some people were probably taught during childhood, while others have learned as adults. However, schools can only teach people as much as they are willing to learn. For example, delivering stand up comedy would not be acceptable while working a funeral. Persistence in such a manner could result in a lost job. Everything has a proper place and a specific audience.

What will it take for you to change less attractive behaviors? How is this accomplished? Less attractive behavior causes people to stand out in a bad way. That may be enough to make some people want to change their behavior, but most of the time people don't change. However, these behaviors can be addressed. We will discuss this a little further in chapter 3. Why might a person want to change? A good reason is because these types of behaviors can cause a person to lose out on various opportunities that life has to offer. Change starts on the inside. I call this the inner being. Your inner being is simply a part of the real you. It's who you really are. You must be able to understand what is appropriate behavior and how and when to use it to maximize your opportunities. Appropriate behaviors and good habits can increase your growth and opportunities. I associate "knowing who you are," with "your inner being," because your inner being encompasses all of the things you are.

Blueprint 2
HOW OFTEN DO YOU?

Have positive thoughts about your life?	N AN S L A
Have positive thoughts about your future?	N AN S L A
Speak positive words about your life?	N AN S L A
Speak positive words about your future?	N AN S L A
Speak positively overall?	N AN S L A
Get along well with your family?	N AN S L A
Get along with your friends?	N AN S L A
How well do you get along with others?	N AN S L A
How well do you get along with strangers?	N AN S L A
How much do you enjoy challenges?	N AN S L A

Blueprint 2

What kind of challenge would you enjoy?
☐ Educational ☐ Physical Why? Explain:

Where have you traveled in the US?

Where have you traveled outside of the US?

Where would you like to travel?

Name one famous person you would like to meet:

If you had the power to help someone else, who would it be and why?

What are your ultimate goals?

Do you know that you will attain your goals?

Do you have any fears about not attaining your goals?

How does this fear affect you?

Principle 2
Plan for the future.

✓ Who? YOU! Life planning is for everyone.

✓ What? Living in the now, but thinking ahead.

✓ Where? Implement change - Access opportunities.

✓ How? Begin to create a blueprint for your life and future.

✓ When? Now, because time waits for no one.

✓ Why? Learning from the mistakes of others.

✓ What? Changing some learned behavior.

Blueprint Notes 2

What areas of your inner being will you work on to enhance?

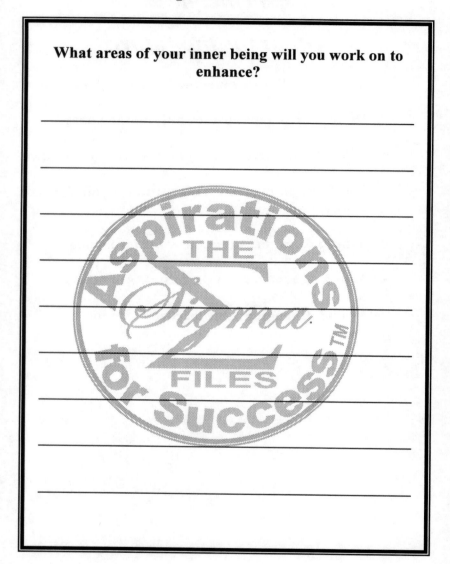

_____

_____

_____

_____

_____

_____

_____

_____

Celebrate Chapter 2

Celebrate your inner being!

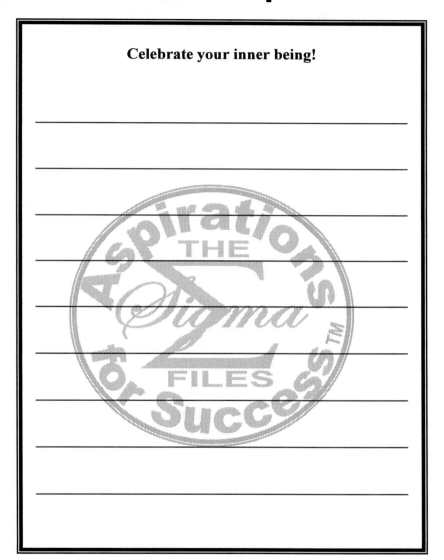

Chapter 3
Outer Actions

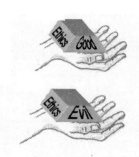

*M*y aunt loves to tell a story about what happened when I was a child and living in Los Angeles. My cousin and I were about 5 years old. Easter Sunday was coming, and I was to have my first solo debut at church. I had practiced my song for weeks and was very excited about the upcoming opportunity to sing before an audience. As far back as I can remember, singing has been one of my greatest passions. Finally the day had come. My cousin was also on the program that day and was called up first to do her Easter speech, which she had also practiced long and hard. As she reached for the microphone, instead of reciting her speech, to everyone's surprise, she began to belt out the words to my song, and she did a pretty darn good job. However, my aunt said that she felt outdone as she looked on from the church pews. My aunt's thought probably went something like this, "what in the world will Linda do now?" However, when I was called upon, I walked to the center stage with the confidence of a young diva, and, unannounced to my cousin, my aunt, or my mother, *I had prepared an encore!*

Somehow, even at an early age, I, as well as most other children, had the ability to find ways to handle obstacles that occur in life. This can happen naturally or it can happen because of the way a child is raised. With the right set of skills and training children, are be able to adapt and handle life's situations just fine, even when resources are limited. The ways in which people respond to challenging situations enable them to build good strong character.

Principle 3: Make good choices

There are great lessons to be learned and many life challenges when making choices -- and the decision that we opt to settle for can lead to success or failure.

Food for thought: Some failures in life are the result of not being prepared and not having a good foundation that steers us toward making good decisions.

In this chapter, we will concentrate on making the best decisions for a healthy and successful future. There's a lot to be said about the choices people make. Whether choices are good, not so good, bad, or just plain ugly, they have lasting impressions on the people they affect. The bad and ugly choices can sometimes hang on for an

> *My philosophy is that not only are you responsible for your life, but doing the best at this moment puts you in the best place for the next moment.*
>
> *Oprah Winfrey*

entire lifetime. Some choices can hold you back from pursuing dreams such as a higher education, a career, and having a full, healthy and happy life. Some bad choices have destroyed people's lives completely. Don't we all hate the bad choices we make? And they're not always easy to fix. Sometimes trying to disguise a bad choice can be as difficult for us as trying to hide or disguise a long bushy tail wagging noticeably from our backside; we can try to stick it inside our pants to hide it, but the bulge will still be seen. That is definitely something you would not want noticed.

Defeat is not the end, but a new start.

Many people are mentally conditioned to accept defeat as the final result, the end, or the TKO punch. I admit it can hurt, but it does not have to be the end. Defeats and failures can be looked on as lessons learned. Once you learn what not to do anymore, you can then focus on what you should be doing. However, some people tend to hang on to defeat. They feel unworthy of success and say things like, "that's just the way it is" or "let's just accept it." Most times people don't know they are conditioned to accept failure as their final result. Because of this, you see people who are very unhappy with their lives, and their unhappiness is reflected in their attitude and their physical body. Although defeat can be emotionally exhausting and even painful, it is up to the individual to make it temporary.

Changing the defeated circumstance never seems to cross the minds of some people. They choose to remain in a state of unhappiness, which is quite unhealthy. It's kind of like watching people who are well, full of potential, with the world at their fingertips. However, they are content to live crammed inside a tiny cage made up of their personal circumstances and drama. The cage door is open, and they are free to go, but they have no desire to leave, even though they are uncomfortable in their present state of living. To add to the madness, their friends and family often follow their self-defeating lead. Sadly, this can be contagious.

Straight Talk about Influences

Do you have people in your circle of influence that could be holding you in a tiny cage? When you look at their success rate, what do you see? If you honestly look into your own mirror, do you see an image of them? Do you walk like them? Have you proudly picked up the same slang language and cute phrases that have gotten them absolutely nowhere? Have you picked up their good and bad habits? Think about this and be as honest as possible. Exactly what do they possess that attracts you? What do they contribute to enhance your life?

I have asked these hard questions to heighten your awareness of the people who are surrounding you. These are the people who have a major influence in your life. So, how much do you really know about the people who are in your circle of influence. What are the people who love you dearly saying about the people in your circle of influence? Are you listening?

Food for thought: *Lend your ears to helpful advice, even if you do not use the advice right away.*

It's hard to see the effects of relationships from a centered view. In the next section or two, you will get a chance to sort out your relationships in the exercises provided for you. These exercises will help you to see relationships from another perspective. You will be able to write down the positive and negative attributes of your relationships.

For example, will the time that you spend with certain people in your life benefit you in the long run? Will it bring you happiness or personal security in any way? Is there a college degree or mentorship connection in store for you out of this relationship? How about a vibrant career or, better yet, the attainment of wealth or some kind of financial security? If you have answered no to any one of these questions, then it is definitely not quantum science from here on out. You need to move on with your life plans and limit the time you are putting into relationships that are stifling you. Sure, we all like to have friends, but be totally honest with yourself about the effects of hanging onto a relationship that is bringing you down. You should form healthy friendships and relationships. Good friendships don't take away from you or your success. Good relationships don't hold you back from attaining your goals. They add richness and happiness to your life. So, don't sell your life plans for cheap. I guarantee that no one will do this for you, so you must do it for yourself.

An example of my relationship evaluation comes from my high school years. It seems like I had plenty of friends in junior high school, but once I arrived at the high school level, my friends formed smaller groups of their own -- and I wasn't included. Although, I still considered them as my friends, I wasn't a part of their smaller groups because I didn't fit in. I didn't participate in the same kinds of activities they participated. And as I look back now, I can see the positive and negative aspects of that occurrence. Through that, I learned how to find better-fitting relation-ships by finding friends with some of the same interests as mine. In this case, it kept me out of trouble. I'm not saying that I never made bad choices, but, for the most part, I learned a valuable lesson about relationships. The relation-ship evaluation that you will soon complete will help you to assess your relationships in their early stages. It's a great tool to use -- if you take the findings seriously.

CIRCLES OF INFLUENCES

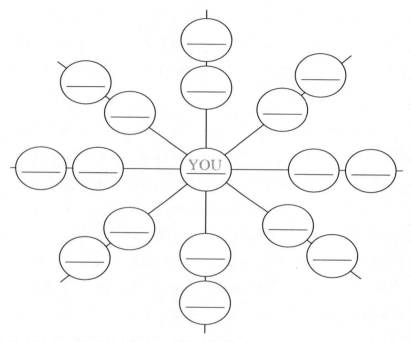

Figure 2: The Circles of Influences

Write your name in the center circle. Write the names of the people you closely associate with in the circles surrounding the center circle. Then in the outer circles, write names and/or titles of people who may be influencing the people who are influencing you. This lesson helps you to visualize how much influence you are receiving. There are both known and unknown influences.

Helping Yourself

Some people desire success, but don't quite know how to attain it. As you create your blueprint, you may find there is indeed a good amount of work to be done. Be encouraged. Just take one step at a time. Once you see your plans on paper from start to finish, you will be able to take action according to those plans. Planning should encompass the goal areas of your life personally and professionally. Planning takes energy, patience and courage. You must have energy because success is not for the lazy. Your level of energy will depend on the state of your mind and body. Your courage and patience will come as you begin to walk the path of success. Those who have already obtained success have found it by doing something for themselves.

On the other hand, when people do nothing with their life and time, there is a much bigger price to pay. Although the price varies with individuals, it could include an empty head, heart, and, depending on where you end up, an empty soul. So, don't become a part of that statistic. Don't wait for a handout or for a hardship to strike in your life before you begin to start your plan. A handout is never as much as you would hope for it to be, and it won't last as long as you would like for it to last.

In retrospect of my life, I write to many of you who could use some inspiration at this point in your life, and perhaps a little push. Equally, I write from my more recent experiences to those who are just starting their lives. I write as someone one who has begun my own personal journey of a successful life. I realize that people must want and accept help in order to be helped. When people want help, they can be helped. But if they refuse, there is nothing anyone can do for them. This is my opportunity to share inspiration and to encourage you to start a plan -- or to move on with your life. It is also my opportunity to empower you with the tools to help you work out some of the details of your journey to success.

As I look at the world as one big picture, I think of humanity as being linked together in many ways. There are family, friends, the people we meet, the people we touch, and those who touch us without ever personally meeting us. Life is one big plan all around us. While talking to people on occasions, I have had conversations related to "planning" in many ways. We've talked about planning a vacation, a wedding, a reunion, but we hardly ever talk about planning a future. In a sense, vacations, weddings, and reunions are life plans. But, for the most part, they are fairly short-lived plans. I mean, you may know where you want to go on vacation next summer, but what about in five or 10 years. If you say you can't think that far ahead, I say yes you can. That is only an excuse. What I'm encouraging you to do is plan for the long run. Why stop at a wedding in two years or a vacation for next summer? What's next? What are you going to do with your entire life? I think you should know.

Stuff Happens

For the most part, it seems that some people just kind of let life happen to them. While in the meantime, when things go bad (as they tend to do when there is no clear direction in life), you may hear those same people say, "stuff happens." While it may be true, stuff does happen, generally LIFE IS WHAT YOU MAKE IT. In the long run, an unplanned life can cost you a lot more than you want to pay, especially while you have the choice. Yes, you do have the choice. You have the free will to make the right choices for life. You see, the way your life goes has a lot to do with the choices you make. Choice is very important. Just remember that a bad choice can leave you up the creek without a paddle.

Taking another look at your behavior pattern is your golden opportunity to think about the world in which you are creating for yourself. What I mean by behavior is, take a look at your actions as well as your interactions. Think about your behavior and how it has affected your relationships. Where has it gotten you this far? If your behavior is not appropriate or needs some adjusting, then it would very much benefit you to work hard in this area to improve. Some people think their bad behavior patterns are subtle enough to go unnoticed; however, although it may not be addressed at that time, it is never unnoticed. With that said, your behavior could hold you back from succeeding. In fact, if you have an unaddressed problem in this area, it can ruin your chances for promotion and advancement opportunities. So, what am I saying to you? "Get your behavior together before it is too late. Your name will follow you for the rest of your life, and your stinking behavior will tag along too."

What kind of world are you creating?

_____

_____

_____

What kind of world would you like it to be in your future?

_____

_____

_____

You are the future. Whatever you create in your world now is how it will be for you later. Sure, people will change, the world will change, but if you don't change, you will more than likely be left behind. You create who you are now, as well as how you want to be perceived by your children, your family and your friends. What value and what kind of lifestyle are you investing in the people who you influence? Later on you will have an opportunity to think about life rewards, because, your payoff is coming sooner than you know. Most people don't think far enough ahead to realize their values and lifestyle can be an investment into the lives of others. Let's take a look at the following diagram to visualize the impact of behavior.

Be Contagious

Uhhh! Say what? Contagious! Yes be contagious. This is in the context of impacting others positively.

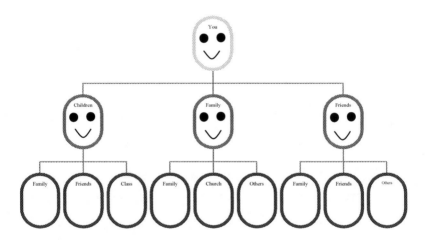

Figure 3: Be Contagious

If you are still conflicted about letting go of things that are detrimental to your success, my question to you is – Ah!! WHY? If you refuse to let go and have reasons why you want to hang on to unhealthy behaviors, friendships and relationships, please feel free to write your excuses here. I will play my imaginary violin while you are writing:

_____

_____

_____

Someone once said, "If you keep doing what you've always done, you'll keep getting what you've always gotten."
OK, are you still having trouble understanding?

Albert Einstein is said to have defined insanity as doing the same thing over and over while expecting different results.

Stumbling Blocks

Stumbling blocks occur from time-to-time to slow or hinder our progress. They always seem to happen when you have taken a few steps in the right direction. Anyone who has succeeded in attaining their goals has probably encountered more stumbling blocks than they would have preferred. At times stumbling blocks may even seem insurmountable. However, you can get over them or go around them. And the good thing is that they can ultimately result in the building of strength and character if you learn lessons as a result of going through them and persevering.

Seeing that life is full of challenges, you should know that a stumbling block can be encountered in many ways. Personally, I have encountered them on a job; through a friendship or relationship; because of a particular habit, attitude or behavior; and all very possibly because of no fault of my own. At different times, while going through life's experiences, I have encountered all of the above – sometimes one at a time, sometimes all at the same time.

Have you ever had a stumbling block to throw you off balance? Some of the most challenging stumbling blocks can decrease your progressive momentum of attaining goals and enjoying life. Nevertheless, keep in mind that things happen for a reason, and sometimes they are beyond your immediate control. I stress this because you are the only one who is responsible for your life results. Therefore, it is important to not let a setback of some kind stop you from moving forward. You are totally capable of learning from stumbling blocks.

Focus on moving forward even through setbacks

Be determined to look forward -- even when things have changed. Make new adjustments to your plans and keep moving forward. At times you will have to determine in your mind to pick up your pace during setbacks and in times of slow downs. Listen and learn to look at the good and bad aspects of the situation in order to learn from the experience. Just remember it is not the end of the road if you say it is not.

Stumbling in relationships

If a relationship is your stumbling block, you probably already know that it is not always easy and it doesn't always go smoothly. Everyone knows that bad relationships can be a huge stumbling block when trying to focus on the attainment of goals. Exactly how can you tell when you are headed into a bad relationship before you get entangled in its web of destruction? Well, it is not very hard to determine this if you pay attention and listen. The problem is that most people don't pay attention or listen. Most people get involved in bad relationships by being willfully blind and ignorant of the apparent signs. I am no relationship specialist, but it doesn't always take a specialist to help a person to see things clearly. Sometimes you can use your life's challenges and lessons as your source of expertise. However, it does require that you be honest with yourself.

It doesn't matter if you are a man or a woman; life has lessons concerning relationships for you. However, it matters very much, when it comes to succeeding at your goals, that you are able to determine which relationships will benefit you or stifle your growth. I have known a few people to get caught up in bad relationships and never rebound.

They were never able to get back on track with their plans for a successful future.

In my youth, I experienced relationships that were both bad and unequal. When I was younger I thought I knew a lot about relationships, but, unfortunately, my character thermostat went only skin deep. What I mean is that a lot of younger people, much like I was, are only able to see the external characteristics of a person -- and they stop with that. If a person is cute or popular, it's a match. Unfortunately, what I didn't know then was that it was an absolute waste of my precious time. That is not the way to form any kind of relationship.

However, through it all, I have learned two things. First off, if you don't have a good sense of who you are and what you want to become, you will more than likely not choose good relationships. Secondly, it's not beneficial if one person in the relationship loves and cares for the other person and has self-respect, but the other person has no self-respect, no discipline, and no self-worth. If this is your situation, these characteristics alone have placed you on a different level than that of the relationship you are in or are about to become a part of. True love (not lust), well-rounded self-respect, and confidence will cause people to carry themselves in a different manner. True love begins on the inside, and it usually causes people to care and respect others.

Being married for several years, I have no big secrets to reveal or magic potions to give you regarding relationships -- other than you must pay attention and weigh the advantages and disadvantages of letting someone in your life. This is not only a wise thing to do, but it is important to your future growth as a person. However, there is one more simple thing that I have learned and would like to share. When someone truly loves you, you won't have to fight for it, you won't have to beg for it, and you won't have to deceive for it. True love has respect, and it won't make you ashamed.

Stumbling while working

On a job, interacting with different people such as bosses, coworkers, vendors, and clients can be a great experience. On the other hand, it can also be filled with many challenges. I have found that one of the best ways to make a working experience become an advantage for me is to have a personal or professional plan that allows me to grow and gain something from the experience. For example, I remember finding a great job that I really enjoyed working. For the first five years, things were going great. I liked working in the professional environment, the pay was okay, the supervisor was good, and the people who I provided support services to seemed to really appreciate my work. Unfortunately, things began to change when my supervisor retired and a new one came onboard. Even so, in the beginning, I looked forward to working for the new supervisor. I didn't foresee any problems because I figured I could adjust to just about any type of supervisor and environment. I had a good attendance record with the company, my work ethic was good, and I had the skills needed to perform my duties. So what could possibly go wrong?

Unfortunately, the supervisor's decision to dislike me created a stumbling block that was beyond my control. Up to that point, I didn't know too many people who didn't like me in the work environment. I used to think that as long as I did my job and steered clear of trouble that I could avoid trouble. However, this was a stumbling block like I had never encountered before. I couldn't run or hide from it. What I didn't know then, but certainly know now, is that conflict between an employee and supervisor is a disaster waiting to happen. From that experience, I learned that people don't always have a reason for disliking someone else. It just depends on the individuals involved. I soon learned to not worry about things that I could not control. Because, in the end, it was up to me to decide how I would respond to this stumbling block.

Nevertheless, this was a huge stumbling block for me. I knew there was nothing that I was going to do to change this person's mind about me. At first I felt like a failure because I really needed the job and didn't want to lose it. However, because of the occurrences, I began to prepare myself for whatever would happen. I also decided to take the experience as a lesson learned. Sometimes life forces us to shift our focus, to wake up, to stop hiding, and to not fear change.

To make a long story short, I would like to say that everything eventually cleared up, and I went on to have a long employment relationship at that company. But, the truth is, I was a goner. However, unknown to me, this stumbling block was about to become one of the best things that had ever happened to me. It forced me to think about securing a better future for myself. I began to see that it was not too late to attain my goals. You see, at that time I didn't even have a degree. Now I am working towards my fourth degree. This stumbling block helped me to take a very important step in the right direction. As for me, there could not have been a better stumbling block to teach me.

What's your personal stumbling block? Is it some action you've taken that you should have thought twice about? Is it a place you shouldn't go ever again? Is it that you need to let go of something that is possibly holding you down? Is it a personal relationship or decision that negatively changed the course of your life? On the next few pages you will have the opportunity to work out some of those choices with the Sigma Relationship Identification. Your documentation can help you to assess your relationships and see exactly where a relationship may be heading. This is a very important step because relationships consume a lot of your time and are a big part of your daily activity. If a relationship is going well, you need to know why. If a relationship is going sour, then you especially need to understand why.

It will allow you to honestly answer some of the hard questions that you may not want to answer out loud. Use them for making those hard decisions about relationships of any kind that could affect you for the rest of your life. Some of the questions may seem a little blunt or cold, but don't count them out. Answer them with honesty and to the best of your knowledge. There is also room at the end of the chapter to add other questions that may also come to your mind.

RELATIONSHIP IDENTIFICATION

SELF

What are your personal values or self-worth/investment?

☐ House/Apartment	☐ Interpersonal	☐ Education
☐ Respect	☐ Nothing	☐ Ambition
☐ Career or Job	☐ Homeless	☐ Self Respect
☐ Ethical	☐ Good Character	☐ Unemployment
☐ Vehicles: _____	☐ Money	☐ Other

What is your education level?

☐ H.S. Drop Out	☐ Certificate	☐ Master's Degree
☐ GED/Diploma	☐ Associate's Degree	☐ Doctorate
☐ Skill Trade	☐ Bachelor's Degree	☐ Other, What? _____

Do you have children?　☐Yes　　☐No　　　How many? _____
How will they be affected? _____

Are you struggling from week-to-week?　　　　☐Yes　　☐No
Is that the way you want to live?　　　　　　☐Yes　　☐No

Do you love or really care for this person?　　☐Yes　　☐No
　　　　　　(ask them to identify the person)
How do you really know? _____

How much?　1　　2　　3　　4　　5　　6　　7　　8　　9　　10
　　　　　　A little　　　　　　　　　　　　　　*A great deal*

What do you want from this person?

☐ Money	☐ Honesty	☐ Love
☐ Physical Relationship	☐ Commitment	☐ Power
☐ Spouse	☐ Children	☐ Time/Attention
☐ Status	☐ Friendship	☐ Other

What are you getting from this relationship?

☐ Finance	☐ Assets	☐ Confrontation
☐ Support	☐ Violence	☐ Mostly nothing
☐ Bills Paid	☐ Grief	☐ Home
☐ Alcohol	☐ True Love	☐ A headache
☐ A good friend	☐ Drugs	☐ Other

What do you give?

☐ Time	☐ Companionship	☐ Attention
☐ Friendship	☐ Money	☐ Love
☐ Support	☐ Conversation	☐ Shelter
☐ Sex	☐ Stability	☐ Advice

Why is this relationship so important to you?

Are you being desperate?　　　　　　　　☐Yes　　☐No

What attracts you to this person?

Have you been completely honest with them about your motives?　☐Yes　　☐No

How well do you know their family and friends? 0 = not at all; 5 = very well

	0	1	2	3	4	5
Mother/Father	0	1	2	3	4	5
Sister(s)/Brother(s)	0	1	2	3	4	5
Relative(s)	0	1	2	3	4	5
Friend(s)	0	1	2	3	4	5

Table 3: Relationship Identification Self

RELATIONSHIP IDENTIFICATION

FRIEND

What is this person's personal value or self-worth/investment?

☐ House/Apartment	☐ Interpersonal	☐ Education
☐ Respect	☐ Nothing	☐ Ambition
☐ Career or Job	☐ Homeless	☐ Self Respect
☐ Ethical	☐ Good Character	☐ Unemployment
☐ Vehicles: _____	☐ Money	☐ Other

What is this person's education level?

☐ H.S. Drop Out	☐ Certificate	☐ Master's Degree
☐ GED/Diploma	☐ Associate's Degree	☐ Doctorate
☐ Skill Trade	☐ Bachelor's Degree	☐ Other, What?

Do they have children? ☐Yes ☐No
How many? _____
How will they be affected?
_____

Are they struggling from week-to-week?	☐Yes	☐No
Are they content with living like this?	☐Yes	☐No
Do they love or really care for you sincerely?	☐Yes	☐No

How do you really know? _____

How much?	1	2	3	4	5	6	7	8	9	10
	A little								*A great deal*	

What do they want from you?

☐ Money	☐ Honesty	☐ Love
☐ Physical Relationship	☐ Commitment	☐ Power
☐ Spouse	☐ Children	☐ Time/Attention
☐ Status	☐ Friendship	☐ Other

What are they getting from being with you?

☐ Finance	☐ Assets	☐ Confrontation
☐ Support	☐ Violence	☐ Mostly nothing
☐ Bills Paid	☐ Grief	☐ Home
☐ Alcohol	☐ True Love	☐ A headache
☐ A good friend	☐ Drugs	☐ Other

What do they give them?

☐ Time	☐ Companionship	☐ Attention
☐ Friendship	☐ Money	☐ Love
☐ Support	☐ Conversation	☐ Shelter
☐ Sex	☐ Stability	☐ Advice

Why is this relationship so important to them?

What attracts them to you?

Have they been completely honest with you about their motives? ☐Yes ☐No

How well do they know your family and friends? 0 = not at all; 5 = very well

Mother/Father	0	1	2	3	4	5
Sister(s)/Brother(s)	0	1	2	3	4	5
Relative(s)	0	1	2	3	4	5
Friend(s)	0	1	2	3	4	5

Table 4: Relationship Identification Friend

RELATIONSHIP IDENTIFICATION, Cont.

HOW OFTEN DO YOU?

Ratings of 1 – 10, 1 None / Never / Little; 10 A lot / Always / Huge / Mostly

You visit them on a weekly basis?	1 2 3 4 5 6 7 8 9 10
They come to visit you?	1 2 3 4 5 6 7 8 9 10
You call them?	1 2 3 4 5 6 7 8 9 10
You respect their lifestyle and decisions?	1 2 3 4 5 6 7 8 9 10
You agree with their opinions?	1 2 3 4 5 6 7 8 9 10
How much of an asset is the relationship?	1 2 3 4 5 6 7 8 9 10
How many problems have they helped you solve?	1 2 3 4 5 6 7 8 9 10
How good is their advice?	1 2 3 4 5 6 7 8 9 10
How important is this relationship?	1 2 3 4 5 6 7 8 9 10
How much overall time do you give?	1 2 3 4 5 6 7 8 9 10

How many warnings have you had that were against this relationship/friendship?

      WHO?   WHY?

1. _____

2. _____

3. _____

Table 5: How often do you?

RELATIONSHIP QUESTIONNAIRE

Briefly describe what is going wrong with the relationship.

_____

_____

_____

What are some of the warning signs?

_____

_____

_____

What lessons have you learned about this relationship?

_____

_____

_____

Did you check out the warning signs?
☐Yes   ☐No   If no, why not?

_____

_____

_____

Do your friends and family approve of this relationship?
☐Yes   ☐No   If no, why?

_____

_____

_____

Can you now move on to a better relationship?
☐Yes   ☐No   If no, why?

_____

_____

_____

Table 6: Relationship Questionnaire

RELATIONSHIP THERMOSTAT

Attractiveness
Hot: ___

Warm: ___

Luke Warm: ___

Cold: ___

Frozen: ___

Trustworthy
Hot: ___

Warm: ___

Luke Warm: ___

Cold: ___

Frozen: ___

Outgoingness
Hot: ___

Warm: ___

Lukewarm: ___

Cold: ___

Frozen: ___

Goals Oriented
Hot: ___

Warm: ___

Lukewarm: ___

Cold: ___

Frozen: ___

TEMPERATURE

Rate the temperature of the relationship.

Hot = Very successful

Warm = Fair/On the Road to Success

Luke Warm = Not too bad/Trying to find self

Cold = Not particularly motivated/Not even trying

Frozen = Forget it

Table 7: Relationship Thermostat

Be honest -- how hot is this relationship?

I hope you have enjoyed the time you have spent working on the relationship identification exercise. You can easily start working on a plan for the future and better relationships when you are able to see the choices you have made or are planning to make, especially when the choices are written out in front on paper. It allows you the opportunity to make sound and rational decisions. These important decisions affect your wellbeing, freedom and livelihood. In this case, with the help of the relationship identification, you can meet the challenges of relationships head-on, just by being honest with yourself about the best choices for you.

Who's really in your corner?

If you are working on improving yourself and becoming the very best you can be, you deserve to find someone whose goal is to do the same. Most people want to find satisfaction, success, love and happiness. They want to be surrounded by other people who care for them and have nothing but their best interests at heart. In fact, finding a satisfying relationship is an important part of life. However, true love and friendship starts with self. If you truly love and respect yourself, you can more easily love and respect others. Therefore, demanding true love and respect is not unreasonable. Likewise, you will be able to identify what is love and care, and what is hate and mistreatment. As a result, you will know when you have found a true friend, a good relationship, and someone who is in your corner.

Where do you go from here?

Some people choose to sleepwalk through life and meet failures and tragedies head-on, even when warned. You can shout, "Hey you, the path you are traveling will meet a dreadful dead-end," and they will still accelerate full speed ahead. Do you know someone like that? It is unfortunate because it hurts the people in their lives who love them the most -- and even worse, it hurts them. They allow anyone and everyone to make the choices for them that sometimes affects the rest of their lives. Choices like how they live, where they live, and how they are treated. Think about it. When the eyes are closed, it's quite difficult to see for yourself where you are going. But, if you really want to know where you are going, you must open your eyes -- the eyes of your heart, mind and soul. You must do this so you can see and read the signs of life.

Don't get me wrong. I am not inferring that this is unintentional. To be willfully ignorant is an intentional act. Blaming your circumstances on everything but your own irrational thinking or bad choices is the coward's way out. You need a wakeup call, and your wakeup call is in this book. So don't stop reading now. You are well on your way to your breakthrough and attaining your goals.

What's missing?

Some people have a missing life link to success, which is simply *a link that you need to connect life chains. It is the one thing you must have in your possession before you can obtain the things in life you want.* You MUST become aware of and accept that the things you do today will affect you in the long run. The choices you make will eventually set a tone for your lifestyle.

In this case, the missing life link is goals setting. Think about this. What would it take to get you moving toward goals setting? If you knew you could have your dream and live your dream by strategically planning to obtain short-term goals that add up to the big goal, wouldn't it be worth doing? Since goal setting is a very important part to success, I have created a goals setting exercise. In this exercise, you will have the opportunity to make a conscious decision that will bring you the most satisfaction and fulfillment. Your goals should be ones that you are willing to commit a frame of time to obtaining.

The goals setting exercise includes keeping a tickler file and schedule of your progress. It will keep you informed of things you need to do to get to your next level. With it you can also work out all of your problems. Sometimes an obstacle can be there because of a lack of information. If you are lacking information, it can be a problem. A lack of information can cause you to be confused about which way to tackle certain situations. But these situations can be worked out. You will find they are easily resolved with the help of these charts. You will get a chance to write down your obstacles and work out solutions that will not only help you, but possibly help others who are going through the same problems. It is a way to document your findings and share the solutions with others. You will see that when you have gathered all of the information you need to proceed and succeed, you will always have it in black and white to refer back to. You can think more logically, and, as a result, make better decisions. The more you document and educate yourself, the more confidence you will gain.

Now, let's take a look at goals setting and start building your plan. The Strategy for Success worksheet and Yearly and Monthly Goals Calendars will help you bring your plans together. The exercises can be used to also help form a strategy that breaks down the plan into smaller workable pieces, and the calendar worksheets can be used for time management.

Plan, Patience, Proceed, Produce.

Blueprint 3

Self Check

Circle Rating: 1 = Not at all; 10 = Very much

Are you proud of yourself? □Yes □No
Rating: 1 2 3 4 5 6 7 8 9 10

Are you proud of your culture? □Yes □No
Rating: 1 2 3 4 5 6 7 8 9 10

What would you make better about yourself, culture or environment?
_____

Do you respect yourself? □Yes □No
Rating: 1 2 3 4 5 6 7 8 9 10

Do you love yourself? □Yes □No
Rating: 1 2 3 4 5 6 7 8 9 10

Are you worthy of success? □Yes □No
Rating: 1 2 3 4 5 6 7 8 9 10

Are you worthy of love? □Yes □No
Rating: 1 2 3 4 5 6 7 8 9 10

Are you worthy of a happy future? □Yes □No
Rating: 1 2 3 4 5 6 7 8 9 10

Do you inspire hope or empowerment in others you meet?
□Yes □No If Yes, How?
_____
_____
_____

If No, Why not?
_____
_____
_____

Blueprint 3

Goals Setting

Type of goal:
- ☐ School
- ☐ Family

    ☐ Business   ☐ Travel
    ☐ Relationship   ☐ Other: _____

What is the goal? Further explain:

_____

_____

Why is it a goal?

_____

_____

_____

_____

What particular need will this goal meet?

_____

- ☐ Employment
- ☐ Family
- ☐ Other:

    ☐ Financial   ☐ Enhancement
    ☐ Association   ☐ Business

_____

_____

Tools Needed:
- ☐ Finance
- ☐ Computer

    ☐ Books   ☐ Transportation
    ☐ Help   ☐ Other: .

_____

Funding Sources:

Professional Resource
Name:

Phone:

Professional Resource
Name:

Phone:

Start Date:

Estimated Cost:

Blueprint 3

Yearly Goals

Goals	Year: 2009	Year: 20___	Year: 20___	Year: 20___
Education				
Career				
Health				
Assets				
Other				
Achievements:				

Goals	Year: 20___	Year: 20___	Year: 20___	Year: 20___
Education				
Career				
Health				
Assets				
Other				
Achievements:				

Goals	Year: 20___	Year: 20___	Year: 20___	Year: 20___
Education				
Career				
Health				
Assets				
Other				
Achievements:				

Goals	Year: 20___	Year: 20___	Year: 20___	Year: 20___
Education				
Career				
Health				
Assets				
Other				
Achievements:				

Blueprint 3

Monthly Goals

	Year: 20___	Year: 20___	Year: 20___
January			
February			
March			
April			
May			
June			
July			
August			
September			
October			
November			
December			

Achievements:

Blueprint 3

Rating Academic Experiences

School Name: _____

Major: _____

Credits Needed: _____ **Estimated Cost:** $_____

Start Date: _____ **Estimated Finish Date:** _____

Year: 20____ Semester: _____			
Class	**Credit**	**Instructor**	**Rating**

Year: 20____ Semester: _____			
Class	**Credit**	**Instructor**	**Rating**

Year: 20____ Semester: _____			
Class	**Credit**	**Instructor**	**Rating**

Year: 20____ Semester: _____			
Class	**Credit**	**Instructor**	**Rating**

Suggested Instructors and Classes	
Class	**Instructor's Name/Phone**

Ratings: 1 = Bad; 5 = Great; Use the suggested section at the bottom to keep track of suggestions from peers.

Principle 3
Make Good Choices.

✓ **Defeat is not the end, but a new start.**

✓ **Straight Talk – who is influencing you?**

✓ **Helping yourself, because it is all up to you.**

✓ **Stuff Happens – But life is what you make it.**

✓ **Stumbling Blocks can be overcome.**

✓ **Who's really in your corner?**

✓ **Where do you go from here?**

✓ **Food for Thought: What is your need and how do you get it?**

Blueprint Notes 3

What did you learn about your outer actions?
What could make your outer actions better?

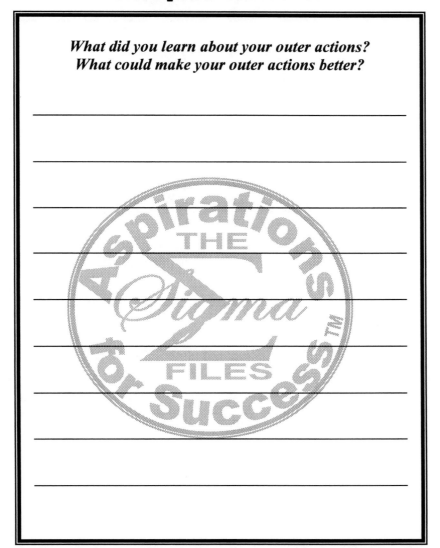

_____

_____

_____

_____

_____

_____

_____

_____

Celebrate Chapter 3

Celebrate your outer actions.

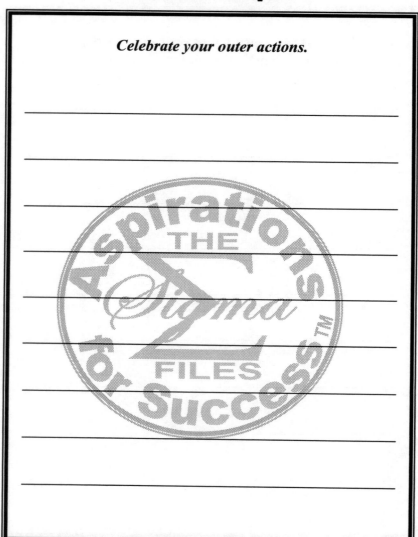

Chapter 4

The Mentor

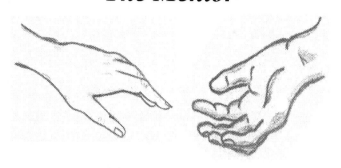

*A*n important link to becoming successful is directly related to how people prepare for success throughout their life. I know that isn't rocket science. However, you are about to read what a best- selling author has written on the subject of the importance of one's preparations. For example, if people think they can and will be successful, they are more likely to plan for success. They are more likely to surround them-selves by successful people and integrate into a positive environment where they can grow. If people choose to take the lazy way out in life and don't plan to have a successful future, they are more likely to surround themselves by the same type of people and in the same type of environment. Thus, they are more likely to attain negative results.

Positive and success driven thinking is always a great asset, but it's also a choice. When it comes to positive and negative actions, only you have the power to select which ones you want in your life. If you decide to consciously choose positive, you'll begin to create powerful and positive results in your life, because the way in which we are programmed will lead to thoughts, which will lead to results. Those are not my words but the words of T. Harv Eker, author of the #1 New York Times best-seller "Secrets of the Millionaire Mind." The formula he uses is called the Process of Manifestation. You may have heard this before. This is how Mr. Eker explains the process:

Our. . .
Programming leads to our. . .
Thoughts lead to our. . .
Feelings lead to our. . .
Actions lead to our. . .
Results that we get.

Process of Manifestation

P	T	F	A	=	R

Table 8: Process of Manifestation

It simply means that the result of our lives is derived from our programming, thoughts, feelings and actions. Because our thoughts, feelings and actions are involved, it allows us an opportunity to change our results or change the outcome of our results by simply changing or modifying our beliefs. Because of this, a person can change and create a successful future. This is done simply by changing the old belief system that does not support the new and successful way of thinking. It's not always an overnight process, but it can be done. It takes understanding and effort.

Some of our beliefs have been with us since childhood. Therefore, the effort to change the way we believe may take a little more time in some cases. It is worth it, especially because it empowers you with choices in how you want to live. Good changes will yield good results, and will drive you toward a higher and more efficient level of thinking, feeling and ways of acting. It is imperative that you are able to fully understand the differences created by, and the effects of, positive and negative thinking and how they influence your results. Once you understand the difference, identify the negative that is controlling your life and begin to modify it and take control of your results and your life.

Over the years, I have noticed that negative thoughts can lead people down the wrong path. Our thoughts are very powerful. But even more importantly, people should identify where negative thoughts originate. Mr. Eker, author of "Secrets of the Millionaire Mind," explains that our thoughts come from programming that occurred while we were growing up. He asks questions like: what kind of things did you hear, see, and experience when you were growing up? Those are the very things that influence your results in adulthood. The same thing goes for success. It is important to become exposed to success and successful people in order to develop a desire to succeed. Exposure can trigger a desire to want and act.

Principle 4: Listen and learn

In chapters 2 and 3 you completed exercises that addressed some of the areas of the inner being and outer actions. From there you have begun to conduct a study of who you are from the inside out. These assessments allow you to see some of the choices you are facing, as well as ones you have already made throughout your life. These choices have affected your life on major and minor levels. However, by studying yourself, you can see that you have the power to make better decisions, and to change your mind about some of the decisions you have made in the past concerning your future. In other words, you don't necessarily always have to play the cards that you were dealt. You, and only you, can choose new cards from the deck in order to enhance your hand.

In saying that, I am hoping you have now begun to put your life plans together. So remain open-minded throughout the remainder of the book; you will see your future both taking shape and in a brighter light.

Mentoring

Mentoring is yet another level to add to the steps to becoming successful. It is important to add a mentor to help you stay on this target. Mentors will give you helpful advice and inspire you to be who you are meant to become. We all should have people who we can turn to for advice -- people we admire for their accomplishments, work ethic, leadership, confidence and strength.

Food for thought: *It is wise to study and listen to others who have already stumbled, walked, or driven down the path of life that you are thinking about traveling. In this you can learn things that can save you time, and perhaps it can save you from headache, heartache and hind-ache.*

Along the way, I have had the privilege of meeting some very successful people -- engineers, doctors and executives -- who have all in some way helped to shape my way of thinking about what I want out of life. It encouraged me to pursue a higher level of education, professionalism and personal growth. However, there are some people who have influenced me, whom I have never personally met. They are people I know only through books, the Internet and television. Nevertheless, they are models from whom I have taken bits and pieces of their great experiences and advice to help me form who I want to become.

You can do it too. Just pick a mentor and write their information on the Mentor Model worksheet and on the opposite side complete your personal information. Use this information to guide you in the right direction. This will help you to keep the focus on your goals and adjust them from time-to-time. Your goal may be to become an astronaut. Having the virtual mentor enables you to choose someone in that field who inspires you.

It is important that you don't allow yourself to become envious or jealous of your mentor's achievements. It is equally important that you don't over extend yourself. This will be unhealthy down the road. So don't allow that to happen to yourself. This is a sure way to fall or stress yourself out unnecessarily. Just keep working according to your plans. Remember that your short-term goals add up in the long run. As long as you are working hard at your goals, you will succeed.

As I mentioned before, you don't necessarily have to have a personal mentor, although it is nice to have one. You can create a virtual mentor by gathering information about someone you admire most. This information should be closely related to your goals. The information you should concentrate on is outlined in the Mentor Model, which will allow you to take a look at your goals and your mentor's achievements. Complete the model by listing the positive attributes from your mentor's life such as educational experience, personal attributes, appearance features, financial success, and public status.

It is okay to set your goals high, but also remember to make your goals realistic and attainable. Let's call it your "strategy for success." From this model you can begin to make up a personal model to help you in creating a plan and a strategy. A strategy is simply a plan of action to pursue a goal; in this case, it's your personal goals. This chart enables you to visualize what is required of you, and it also helps you to address the timeline for meeting your goals. With the help of the chart, you will be able to break your strategy down in time frames that will allow you to pursue them in segments. As you will see, the Mentor Model and the planning strategy are interrelated. Together, they focus simultaneously on your aspirations for success and future achievements.

Blueprint 4

The Mentor Model

Your Name:	Mentor Name:
Educational Goals:	Educational Achievements:
Career Goals:	Career Achievements:
Personal Style Goals:	Personal Style:
Activity/Hobby:	Activity/Hobby:
Associations/Clubs:	Associations/Clubs:
Strengths/Characteristics:	Strengths/Characteristics:
Other Attributes:	Other Attributes:
Comments:	Comments:

Fill in the first column that is designated for your information. Then select a mentor and fill in the second column with information that describes the positive attributes that inspire you about your mentor. Use this information as a guide to inspire you to achieve your goals. This mentor can be someone you know personally or someone you don't know. For example, what inspires you? Is it personality, educational achievements, personal appearance, career achievements, hobbies, and/or strength?

Please don't get me wrong. This is in no way preferred above having a personal mentor, but it can be used in coordination with a mentor. Remember, it would be ideal for you to have a personal mentor. This is only a substitute if there is no one ready, willing or able to support you. If this is your reality, you can create a virtual mentor. You don't have to be discouraged. The Mentor Model is a great tool to help you put your virtual mentor in place. Mentorship is a powerful interactive resource. It allows people to meet others who can add growth and wealth to another person's life. Mentors inspire hope and determination. If you want to know why it is important to choose a mentor or a virtual mentor, the answer is simple. Everyone should have someone to look up to and to receive helpful advice and receive encouragement from someone who is easily accessible. It takes everyone working together to make a difference in this world, and a good mentor will certainly make a difference in the life of someone else. In a few words: it is not only our families who can shape our lives. There are many other people who can add to our personal and professional growth. The fact is that we can use the journeys of other successful people as a compass to guide us anywhere we want to go.

There are many mentors such as spiritual leaders, counselors, teachers, other professionals, and also famous people who can all add an abundant wealth of knowledge to our lives. As I said before, it would be ideal to have a personal mentor, but there is no rule that states you can't use a virtual mentor to help map your journey. All you need to know is: How did they achieve their goals? What can I learn from their experiences? How can I achieve mine? Remember to be very positive when selecting a mentor.

Do not use this exercise to pick apart another person's flaws.

Do not use the model to measure your goals against someone else's unjustly.

Simply choose the positive attributes about a person that inspires you and take the time to put in place your own solid plan. Don't make yourself sick trying to aim too high or doing things too fast or all at once. Simply pace yourself; you will get there. That is what blueprinting is all about. It's a plan for building. Make a long-term plan and break it down into short-term plans that you can reach over time.

Principle 4:
Listen and learn.

✓ **Look, Listen, and Learn.**

✓ **Make choices that are consistent with your love and respect for yourself.**

✓ **Help yourself to succeed. Think about it. What can you do?**

✓ **Become a mentor.**

✓ **Be honest. Create better relationships.**

Blueprint Notes 4

How important is mentorship to you?
Who can you mentor?

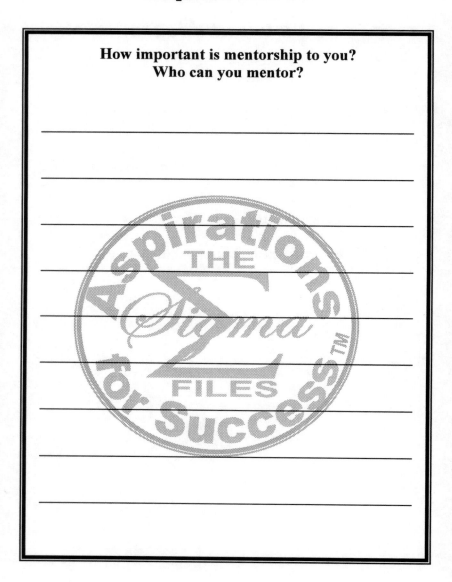

Celebrate Chapter 4

Celebrate your journey!

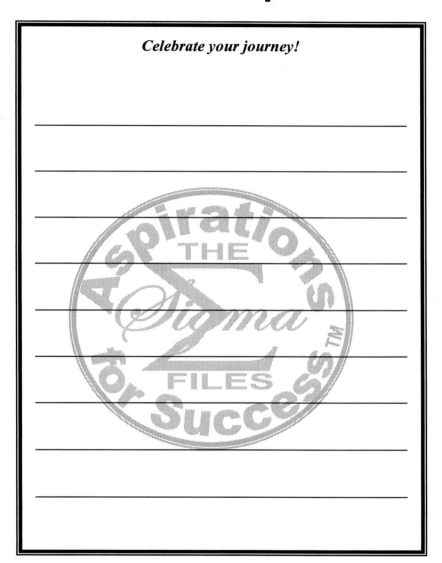

Chapter 5

Get in the Competition

*W*hy do some people succeed at reaching their goals while others fail? The answer lies within all of us individually, yet there is a common answer. It's the same answer we touched on previously. You must have a plan, a strategy, and the ability to execute your plan in incremental time frames. To not have a plan for your future is to leave yourself open to possible failure.

Some people were fortunate enough to dream of their success and rise from their dreams excited and motivated. At that point, they were ready to take on the world. These fortunate individuals were able to share their hopes and dreams with their family and friends who in return encouraged them at an early age to prepare to reach their goals.

Other people who are now successful also realized their potential at a point in their lives early enough to make preparations. Preparing for a successful life starts way before success is realized. That is the key to turning hopes into reality.

I encourage you to dream big too. In addition, I hope you will remember your dreams for success once you have awakened. Turn them into plans, strategy, and then reality. Wake up with excitement about the possibilities of a bright future in this huge world of opportunities. Set goals that reach beyond your inner circle. Set goals that will keep you inspired, and ones that will challenge you personally and professionally. Set goals that can reach out to your community and to the world around you. Believe in yourself and speak positive affirming words each day as you go about reaching your goals. Say to yourself, "I am capable, and I am committed to having a well planned and successful future." It doesn't matter what city or town you grew up in, these simple principles can help you reach your goals. They are universal principles that work for us all.

Reviewing the principles:
1. Get to know yourself.
2. Plan for the future.
3. Make good choices.
4. Listen and learn.

Embrace this opportunity to focus on your life. You only have one life to live. May these words inspire urgency within your heart and mind to do the right things for your future. Really find yourself in the assessments and exercises. Study and challenge yourself to understand your situation and the things that have brought you to this point in your life. If you have made wise choices, that's great! I applaud you! You have accomplished something fantastic. However, if you see some things about your life and the choices you have made that you would like to improve, now is your chance to work through these issues. Sometimes you can avoid making some of the same mistakes you have made previously if you only look at them from another perspective. Blueprinting helps to give you another perspective. With the help of an additional perspective from blueprinting, you can actually see your plan of action and begin to own up to the reasons you have taken the path you have chosen. The truth is, when you understand who you are and where you have come from, you will be able to differentiate the path to where you are headed, from the path to where you would really like to go. It is imperative, especially at this time of life.

Principle 5: Expect great results

Would you like to get into the game of life? Have you noticed there are a lot of players in this game? In this game, some of the players are movers and shakers in your towns, cities and communities. You may see them as heads of organizations, on television and radio, and doing various other jobs in your town. These incredible people set policies, teach children, patrol the streets, create jobs, and empower communities. And guess what? They are also there to help you get to where you want to go. Just like in "The Mentor" chapter, be aware that these people have a wealth of knowledge to share with you. Principle 5 states "Expect great results." Well, these people are there to help you obtain great results. In return, they are expecting something great out of you. Certain people have planned out their day to spend time talking to you, teaching you, counseling you, helping you, and motivating you to become your very best. Make sure their time spent with you is not wasted. Be sure to make the most of it.

Food for thought: Have you ever thought about the reason why teachers, counselors and advisors encourage others to make the right choices for their future? Well, it is not for the teacher's benefit that this happens. These people already have their education and careers. They teach and encourage for the benefit of their students. They understand that people such as students have great potential. They know that the abilities that lie within a student's mind is the potential to make their lives better and to touch other people's lives in ways that most students can hardly imagine. Teachers try hard to get students to see this for themselves and to believe it.

It begins with respect

To have self-respect is a valuable characteristic. It is up to each person to have the proper respect for self and for the things that can be accomplished. I asked several young adults to share with me their meaning of self-respect. I received some very interesting answers. Although, I admit that some of the answers were odd and some were mis-guided, and a few of the answers leaned more towards having pride than respect, there were a few young people who hit the target with their answers. However, out of almost all of the young adults who I asked this question, we were able to agree that self-respect and confidence together will take them much farther than pride. Self -respect and confidence are a part of the inner being and is evidenced by outer actions. True self-respect goes beyond race, color, creed, culture and welfare. Most times self-respect is learned at an early age. However, people have the ability to learn to love self and to gain self-respect; they can also learn to love and respect others. Now that's something in which people can possess the right kind of pride. The level of respect will show up in every part of life, especially in areas that are thought to be insignificant.

What does it mean to have self-respect?

_____

_____

_____

Do you have self-respect? If so, how is it evidenced?

_____

_____

_____

What do you expect from yourself and others?

_____

_____

_____

Expectation is a good motive for making plans. So what do you expect? Do you expect to have a great career one day? Do you already have a career and expect to grow within the organization for which you currently work? Well, how are you going to get there? In order to have a great career, you should consider going to school, getting some training, and/or gaining knowledge and experience. You can start from the bottom and gradually work your way to the top. Do you expect to buy a home, travel, go to college, or be healthy? All of these things are expectations, and they all take planning and effort.

I was picking up food for a meeting for about 15 people at a restaurant one afternoon, and as I waited for my order, I engaged in conversation with the cashier behind the counter. As we discussed the subject of career planning, she told me that she would one day like to own a restaurant much like the one in which she was working. I told her that she was in a great position to learn about the business and suggested that she work her way up through the different positions. She had a great opportunity to learn the industry firsthand.

I could see from her enthusiasm that she was honestly excited about the possibilities of her future. At the end of our conversation, as I proceeded to leave, I asked her for plastic-ware to go with my order. She was very gracious and responded by giving me a serving for approximately 60 people or more. She literally grabbed a couple of handfuls of plastic-ware and placed them into a bag for me. I quickly realized her good intentions, but, as a business graduate, I couldn't help but seize the opportunity to give her a simple lesson in how businesses make a profit. I kindly explained that making a profit is the goal of every business owner. It is directly related to the total operation of a business, which also includes the careful distribution of supplies. One day, when she owns her business, I hope she will benefit from this little piece of information.

Respect: Big Effort – Big Reward

- If you expect to become someone of great character and strength, you will be.

- If you expect people to respect you, you must gain their respect. This is done through the formation of trusting relationships.

- If you expect your employees to work hard and provide great customer service, you must work hard and be committed to extending good customer service.

Think about where you are in your life right now and where you would like to be in a few years from now. Are your plans in line with your expectations? Will your expectations for your future affect your family members and friends in a positive or negative manner in any way?

Putting your best foot forward

What position do you currently play in the game of life? When you have assessed your role, it will tell you exactly how much competitive advantage you have both personally and professionally. Do you know what it means to have a part in the game of life? If you don't know exactly what it means, that's okay. I will try to break it down in this chapter as you read on.

As you begin to make plans for your future and meet your goals, think about where you want to be and what role you will play in your family, your community or on your job. Again, in order to get into the competition, you must have an advantage over others -- whether it is a skill, a talent, and/or education.

To get into the game of life, you must find your personal and professional competitive advantage and ensure it is above or very closely comparable to that of others. This is how you put yourself in a winning position. If you want to be considered for anything -- a career, a promotion, a professional sports position -- you must have something to offer personally and/or professionally.

Having the competitive advantage is a term that is heavily used in the business community. However, in this context, it simply means to have a strategy that

> *It ain't as bad as you think. It will look better in the morning.*
> *Colin Powell*

enables you to compete in life and win. Yes! Having a competitive advantage can put you in the competition and enable you to win!

Competitive change and growth

Knowing and thinking about the competition today, and being prepared to compete today, are two different things. The demands of the economy have increased. The demands of people and employers have increased. And as a result, the planning of your future needs to change to meet these demands. This could require you to set your perimeters to exceed the needs of the demands, thereby creating a personal/professional competitive advantage. It is up to you to determine your area of competition by finding out what it is and what you are up against. Then you can add skills, abilities, and positive characteristics that enhance your chances for success. This includes education, training, communication, and personal appearance. Speaking of appearance, it's very important to fit into an environment and not to over or under compensate.

We live in a competitive world. In a lot of cities, the job market has slowed considerably. It is challenging to find jobs that offer full time work and benefits. Unemployment has increased, and the demand for skills and experience has expanded. Specialized skills, international competition and globalization have taken front stage. Because of this, you will need to adjust your personal and professional attributes. A good question to ask is what personal and professional attributes you have to offer above the attributes of others in a particular field?

Personal Growth

Although I spend a lot of time compelling younger people to start planning, people of all ages can use the principles as a guide for personal growth. As I think about the times in my past when I struggled and the times when I lacked motivation, I can remember some of the faces of people who crossed my path. Some of them never did find themselves. They seemed to have gotten lost in time. Some of their lives ended tragically, and some of them just never seemed to live up to their potential.

When I was a junior in high school, a classmate of mine telephoned one evening to inform me that he had decided against returning to school. I knew he was head-strong in school and could never quite get it together. He rarely listened to the teachers or his parents. The bottom line is that he just did not do what needed to be done academically to comprehend at the grade level he had been promoted to. I still remember pleading with him to rethink his decision, but, to no avail. However, I still didn't fully understand what would lead him to make such a bad decision. He had come to his 11th year, with only one more to go before receiving the reward. Sadly, my friend never made it back to school. I would love to end this story by writing about his many accomplishments afterward, but the truth is that he had a very hard life thereafter. After my graduation, I frequently saw him walking the streets of downtown peddling whatever he could get his hands on. Eventually, I read that his life ended sad and homeless on those very streets.

You may be someone who already has a decent handle on the educational process and the requirements for getting a good job and career. You may have a strong mind and will to succeed, but what if your attitude stinks? Perhaps you are headstrong and refuse to listen to people who can help you. You may be a great person, but you do not listen well to others who are there to help you. Perhaps you have a problem with authority figures. If so, I am pleading with you today. Don't go down that same road of destruction that many others have unsuccessfully traveled. In fact, you have just read about one particular story out of millions that could be told.

- How do you handle taking orders and constructive criticisms?

- What kind of boss do you want to become?

A person's belief can be a controlling factor in their behavior and response. We discussed this in Chapter 4 when we looked at the Process of Manifestation. In order to gain personal advantage, those are the areas of study that you can take a look at. The following diagram may be of assistance in helping you formulate a list of your positive attributes. I encourage you to review the following chart. Really think about how you want to grow personally and make plans to do so today.

How do you obtain personal growth? There are various resources to help along the way. You can ask people, read books and education materials, go to seminars, or search the Internet, just to name a few. It is not complicated. You should always aim to better yourself. It takes practice, honesty, time and commitment. The empowerment of personal growth will make you feel great and put you in the competition.

Blueprint 5

Comparisons Between Personal Advantages and Disadvantages		
	Advantages	**Disadvantages**
Characteristics	Positive attitude, honesty, caring, dedicated, team worker, hardworking, self motivated	No self-control, gossip, backstabbing, lazy, tardy, unorganized, rude
Body Language	Energetic, attentive, a firm hand shake, convey confidence, willingness, enthusiasm, aggressiveness	Speaks so low it is hard to decipher, rudeness, harshness, over compensation, rolling eyes as if to say "whatever," lazy, slouchy
Appearance	Is your appearance fresh? Polished shoes, appropriate attire, standing out inappropriately, under/over compensate	*Street clothes – fads and fancies are not appropriate for every occasion. **Loudly colored hair. Slouchy, stained clothes
Conversation	Ability to articulate well, knowledgeable about subject matter, respectful	Profanity, gossip, resentful responses, inappropriate comments
Etiquette	Knowing what is acceptable in the workplace	Doing what is not acceptable. Bad habits that affect others in a negative manner
Actions	Team worker, completes individual projects, uplifting	Does not work well with others, acts without thinking, hurtful to others
Ethics	Hardworking, does what's right, makes good choices, respectful	Self-seeking, evil, unwilling to do what is right
Conflict Management	Ability to handle pressure, receives constructive criticism well, resolves issues	Easily provoked to anger, confrontational, hard to satisfy
Friends	Being a leader, helping others grow, inspiring	A follower, just fitting in
Results	Happiness, satisfaction, maturity, becoming a mentor, high rate of success, prosperous	Anger, displacement, unanswered questions, immaturity, low success rate, broken, destitute, sad

*   *If you look like you are going to the movies, on a date, to the grocery store, etc. – it is not appropriate for an interview.*

**   *Not fitting in a professional office, but may be fitting in a bar.*

Professional Growth

When you begin to gain the advantage in your personal life, you will begin to see how you can obtain the advantages in areas of your professional life. A long-lasting professional career is dependent on  your ability to grow professionally. One way to grow professionally is through education and training. Education is twofold, in that it opens the door to finding a suitable career and maintaining it. I'm not saying that your adult success always has to include advanced education or that education is the only way to gain professional growth, although it is a great asset and will broaden your intellect, however, I am saying that you most definitely need some kind of high school diploma and experience. Furthering your education is an additional advantage, and it will allow you far more opportunity. So, if you have goofed off a little, now is the time to wake up and smell the coffee.

Professional growth is important to the longevity of your career. Companies and businesses are run by individuals who possess certain levels of talents, skills, and abilities to oversee the continual growth of the company. Large corporations are headed by the top competitors. To find your own professional competitive advantage, you must learn from these types of individuals. Learn what you need to know about the business or field that you would like to enter, and not only obtain the talents, skills, and abilities needed for entry, but work toward obtaining the extra edge that sets you apart from others. It takes more than just a pretty smile or face to compete in the career market today.

Do a thorough investigation on what is needed for you to compete in your respective field. Start by making a checklist of requirements that you will need in this field. Study the list and strategically plan how you will obtain the requirements. Then write another list of extra special attributes that will ensure you gain the competitive advantage.

For example, having an educational degree, experience, special skills, ethical behavior, and an outstanding attitude are just a few attributes that will set you apart from others. Write out any additional skills, education, experiences, and so forth.

Blueprint 5

Comparisons Between Professional Advantages and Disadvantages		
	Advantages	**Disadvantages**
Goals	To set marks of achievement in your future. Create life circumstance	To do nothing, life happens, to take no responsibility
Achievement of Goals	To reach the mark you set. Career, education, winner, opportunities	Does not have a goal or know what it is. Low pay, low self esteem, need assistance
Education and Knowledge	To be able to competitively compete in the market of one's expertise; credentials	Minimum education, minimum training, no expertise
Outlook	To have a bright outlook for future opportunities, learning, growing, unlimited goals, great attitude	Pessimistic, dim, dark, blames others, wasted time, cycle to nowhere, limited, at a standstill
Skills	Experience, training, specialty, commits to challenge	Minimum, below entry level, lacking in personal growth
Style	Always appropriate, able to conform if needed. Conservative, a winner	Inappropriate, stand out, inability to conform, hang with losers
Conflict Management	Ability to handle pressure, receives constructive criticism as a tool for growth, ability to resolve issues, problem solver	Easily provoked to anger, confrontational, hard to satisfy, problem finder, have no solutions
Career	Create options, chance to advance	To take whatever is offered
Results	Happiness, satisfaction, maturity, full of life, high rate of success, prosperity	Anger, displacement, depleted and defeated, immaturity, low self esteem, broken, destitute, sad

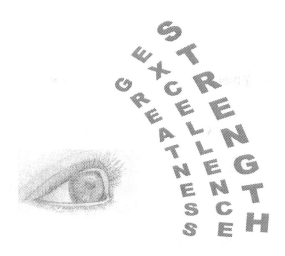

Figure 4: Visualizing Achievements

Visualizing Achievements

Planning your goals and educating yourself takes time and work, and that takes patience. Begin to visualize what it will take for you to attain your goals. A healthy visualization will help make the time and work worthwhile. Take the time to enjoy each and every one of your achievements. Commit to your vision -- you will eventually have it. You will find your purpose, your place in life, when you begin to actively visualize your journey. It is about being confident enough to stand up and pursue the things you want out of life. This is an important part of your planning and education process. This is called visualizing your achievements.

Think it, feel it, see it, and do it!

I encourage you to write down the questions that come to your mind. Start by thinking about what you would like to achieve, and how you plan to achieve it. I challenge you to think big for long-term goals, but, remember to break them down into smaller short-term goals. You owe it to yourself. Imagine it, write it, see it, and then put it into action. Write down the positives and negatives of your journey. Why the negative? Writing the negative things down will help you to see what obstacles you may need to overcome and learn from in order to move on to the next step. As for the positives, embrace them. Once you begin to see the entire picture, you will find yourself ready to take on new challenges, jump over obstacles, and run through the barriers that are presented. Get inspired. After all, it is your life.

VISUALIZING GOALS

You must be able to visualize your goals and incorporate balance into your life as you pursue them. Write in the spaces below all of the attributes/achievements you are planning to accomplish with your hands, feet, mind, etc. For example, with my hands, I plan to write a book. So, in one of the spaces write "book" if you plan to author one, write "house" if you plan to buy a house or "land," if you plan to buy property, or "travel" if you'd like a trip to Paris," etc.

Visualizing His Goals   **Visualizing Her Goals**

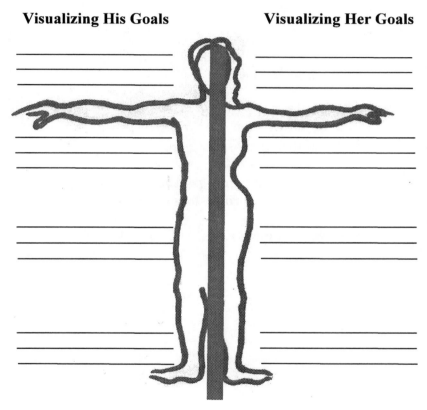

Figure 5: Visualizing Goals
This diagram will help you visualize the various areas of your personal goals. If you can see these areas, you can put your goals into perspective from your head to your feet.

Principle 5:
Expect great results

✓ **What do you expect from yourself? What do you expect from others? What do you expect out of life?**

✓ **Change and Growth**

✓ **Personal Growth**

✓ **Professional Growth**

✓ **Visualizing Achievements**

✓ **Review the advantages and disadvantages of personal and professional growth.**

✓ **Visualizing your goal.**

Blueprint Notes 5

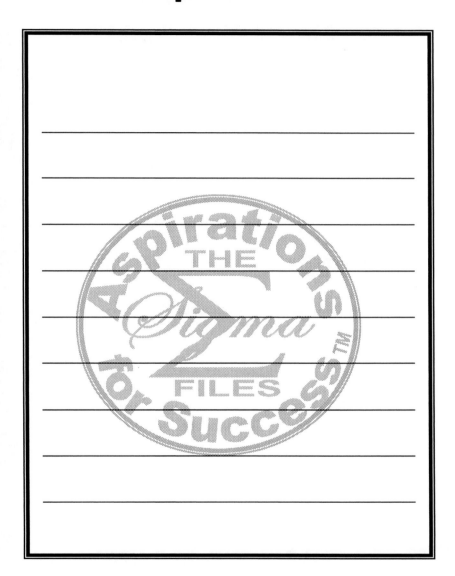

Celebrate Chapter 5

Celebrate your will to win!

Chapter 6
Building a Legacy

*E*ach chapter adds another level to the completion of your personal blueprint.

- Chapter 1: Who Are You? Focuses on the importance of knowing oneself. History is important.

- Chapter 2: Inner Being - Is a look at personal characteristics and a reminder that when people plan their future, they plan to succeed in the future.

- Chapter 3: Outer Action – Is a reminder that who you are influences your inner being, which influences your outer actions. In addition, people play an important role in your success, believe it or not.

- Chapter 4: The Mentor – Invites you to choose mentors who inspire you to go beyond the norm of what you may think you can do or beyond negative messages that you may have received in the past.

- Chapter 5: Get in the competition — encourages you to stop sleep walking through life. Some of the actions you are taking may never prepare you to have the personal competitive advantage. Therefore, if you persist, you will surely lose out on a lot of opportunities.

Principle 6: Commitment and endurance is the key to obtaining success.

Building a legacy is by far the most important chapter in this book. Well, OK! I may have said this somewhere before, but, be assured that the building of your personal legacy is as important as knowing your

> *We allow our ignorance to prevail upon us and make us think we can survive alone -- alone in patches, alone in groups, alone in races, even alone in genders.*
> *Maya Angelou*

history. Honestly, throughout this entire book you have been given many opportunities to add value to your life and build a legacy for yourself, your family, and your friends. A legacy doesn't only consist of a monetary inheritance; it can be of other extrinsic value such as physical gifts, benefits, and anything else that is rewarding to you. Yes, building your legacy will bring you great self-respect and joy.

Setting up the reward

Some people may not think in terms of setting up rewards on a daily basis. However, don't be mistaken; there are many people who have thought on the subject of setting up rewards for themselves and for their family. They are strategically planning and building their legacy. A legacy will allow you to say who you are and how you want to be known. Legacies are powerful in that they usually outlast the people who created them.

Food for thought: No matter what you might think, some legacy is being attached to you. Your legacy is being built every day from the things you do and the things you don't do to prepare for your future.

Ask yourself if the things you are doing will be of value to you or those you love. To take a look at what value lays in the things you love doing, consider the following questions:

- Am I creating a future I will be proud of?

- Why am I doing the things I do?

- What am I gaining from doing these activities?

- What kind of influence does it have on others?

- How and to whom am I accountable?

I want to make this very clear to you. You will be held accountable for the things you do. It could be family, friends, or even people you don't know personally. Accountability should be a key factor in your process to establish your legacy. Just know this, no matter what stage of life you are living in, you can begin to build a legacy that is worth passing on -- and one in which you won't be ashamed to be associated.

Let's approach the subject of creating a legacy in terms of gift giving. Has anyone ever given you a gift? It could have been money, jewelry, time, or attention. Just think about this. Legacy is your gift to give. That's the great thing about having a personal legacy. You can present it in your own style. You may be someone of great character, have high standards, and lots of class -- or you may be someone who wishes to improve style in the certain areas. It really doesn't matter because it's the thought of gift giving that is important. If you give from your heart, it will be appreciated, and it will repay you a great reward.

Write down a list of things that will create personal value and legacy in your future. Call it your legacy list. Remember, this legacy list should contain long-term goals in which you can continue to build on: such as teaching and entrepreneurship. Think about the ways in which you affect other people's lives right now. Then think about how you would like to touch their lives. Weigh the good and not-so-good ways you affect others. What do you want people to know about you? What gift or what part of yourself could you give to your own family that they will carry forward?

Legacy List

Use this space to document any opportunities that you see to help you create and build your legacy. For example: writing a book, a poem, a song, opening your own business, a franchise, volunteering, etc. Also, explain what value it will be to your future.

1. _____
2. _____
3. _____
4. _____
5. _____
6. _____
7. _____
8. _____
9. _____
10. _____
11. _____
12. _____

Table 9: Legacy List

False Pride

A young man once told me an interesting story about his life when he was growing up. He had memories of his childhood potential being hindered before it had a chance to flourish. Because of this, he ended up with a false sense of pride, a lazy work ethic and destructive habits that almost consumed him in his early adulthood. He believes the reason for some of his failures in his adult life stemmed from his life as a child – that because he was raised with practically no discipline in his life, the beginning of his adult life started in shambles.

Food for thought: *A molehill of issues can soon turn into a mountain of problems.*

This young man was very handsome and quite talented, which is something that he was aware of at an early age. His good looks gave him a sense of pride. However, sadly as he reminisced about his life, he also expressed a sense of insecurity and deep regret as he talked about the time he wasted on his good looks alone.

According to him, when he was growing up, he didn't have to work very hard to get what he wanted from others. His good looks bought him many favors. In school, if he didn't want to do something, he simply turned on the charm. Now, however, he realizes he swindled and squandered his way through school on good looks and class clowning, despite being constantly warned by his teachers and peers.

In junior high school, he began experiencing problems that were beyond his usual solution of good looks and class clowning. He noticed his reading and math skills were not at the level of some of his classmates. All of a sudden, the tables were turning, and he began to feel the after-effects of falling behind and not taking his education seriously. Although he was able to maintain the minimum grades that barely kept him moving to the next grade level, he knew within himself that his problem was growing out of hand, and that made him insecure. Although he conveyed a hard outward appearance, within he felt ashamed of his situation. It had gotten hard for him to keep up with his school work, and he didn't have the work ethic to motivate him to try harder. It was at this point that he felt hopeless, so he hid his shame by choosing to increase his level of goofing off and acting out in front of his classmates. His embarrassment began to consume him, and it eventually turned to anger. As a result, he was furious with his parents and the school system for reasons he didn't quite understand.

In high school he noticed his good looks were still there, but they were certainly not enough to get him by anymore. Most of the favors he had gotten in his earlier years had subsided. Up to that point, he had taken it for granted that he didn't have to want for much, because things were always done for him. Nevertheless, he could no longer hide his insufficiencies behind his good looks. It was apparent to everyone who encountered this young man that he had some issues and was not being true to himself.

Although this may not be your story, it may resemble a familiar one that you know of. Perhaps the issue is not looks – but maybe it's gender or weight or color, or something similar. If so, it's because this kind of situation happens almost every-day to people we know and care about. You may know of someone who needs help and appears to be trying to hide their insecurities. If so, encourage that person to get help before desperation sets in. There is absolutely no reason for anyone to be ashamed. If they are still in school, encourage them to get the help they need while it is available.

The things you learn or do not learn during your early edu-cation will affect you for the rest of your life. Many students are behind in their reading and math skills and feel trapped and helpless. Some students may think there is no other solution, or that it is too late to get help because they're so far behind. Other people let pride get in the way of their success. Remem-ber help is always available, and there are plenty of people with enough compassion to stop and take notice.

When my friend was younger, one of his greatest fears was that he would settle for an unmotivated or substandard way of living. His living environment and friends welcomed it. In fact, some of his friends had already settled into this kind of lifestyle. However, this young man finally began to reach out for help. It wasn't always easy for him. Relearning was quite a challenge. In the process, he improved his reading and math skills, and later he earned a college degree. His dream was to become a professional model. With some planning and dedication, he did that and much more. Now his greatest hope is that he can encourage many others to plan to be successful and to not let fears and past failures stop them from moving forward in a positive direction.

No more excuses.

When talking to people, I often hear excuses as to why things haven't worked out for them in life. Such things as: I'm not college material, I failed my biology class twice, it will take me five long years to get a degree, and so on and so forth. However, my response to them is to find something else to do - - get a skill, take the biology class a third time, or other positive words. Making the right decisions for your life will not always be easy. It takes commitment and endurance but is well worth the effort. Obtaining an education and skills will grant you many opportunities that may be otherwise lost.

Planning to reach your goals by writing your goals down is a very important step, and by now you should be able to clearly see the importance of surrounding yourself with people who are supportive, success driven and positive. Again, finding these individuals will give you the opportunity to integrate into a positive environment, and to have a well-rounded learning experience from people who are like minded. Learning stimulates enthusiasm and inspiration. In my experience, meeting successful people helps to reshape thinking about life and goals. It encourages people to pursue higher education, professionalism and personal growth. You will find this to be true for you as well.

Rewards

You only get one life to make an impact, and this is your time to shine. SO MAKE IT BIG! The building of your legacy is being constructed throughout all six chapters. This is not an easy process. It takes long and careful thought and consideration. It is a process that makes you think before you make a move that will affect your future. But, just think how proud you will be when you experience the rewards of building a successful life and legacy. Use the creativity in your own mind. Remember, you are needed, you are important, and you are capable of succeeding -- so find your area of expertise. You are a part of your community and a part of this world. So what are you waiting for? It's time to stop crying and whining because someone may have done you wrong or because things are not going just right.

Your results will be satisfying, and they will determine your rewards. Do it for yourself, your family, a friend, a neighbor, or perhaps other people in your community who also need to improve their quality of life? You are on your way to becoming an individual of positive impact. By investing into yourself, you subsequently invest in the lives of those you love and into the lives of those you may never know. Some people didn't have positive influences in their lives; but now they have you. By taking a stand, you encourage others to follow your lead. This will have a lasting effect on their lives. Just know that you owe it to yourself to move forward, and it is within your power.

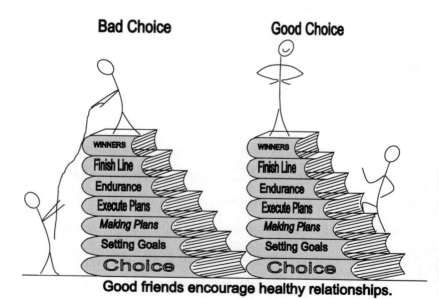

Good friends encourage healthy relationships.

Figure 6: Choices

Can you think of someone who needs encouragement? Perhaps it's a neighbor, a friend, a coworker, or the child next door. There are a lot of negative things going on in communities these days. You hear about them in the news and read about it in newspapers. Local non-profits and other organizations are at capacity trying to meet these needs. For some organizations, it is almost overwhelming. It's going to take every one of us joining together to effect a positive and long lasting change in our communities, as well as in ourselves. Perhaps you know of someone who needs proper guidance. Some people are wrongly influenced by what they see in the media. Some of them may carry themselves in an improper manner or, worst, they could be prone to making bad choices for themselves because of low self-worth or low self-esteem. It's amazing how many people go on about their lives and do not consider helping others around them. The truth is that the situations and solutions that affect your neighborhoods and communities originate from individual actions and participation, which leads to group involvement. You are not in this world alone. Your contributions, whether they are big or small, wrong or right, do matter. We are all in this world together for a reason. It takes positive people to effect positive change, leaders, investors, caregivers, and all of those who are willing to teach, listen and support each other.

By stepping up to the plate in your situation, your town, your school, or your relationships, and reaching out to others, you become the mentor model you saw in Chapter 4. The greatest part about this process is that you will be able to show others how they too can make plans for their future.

Personal Reward

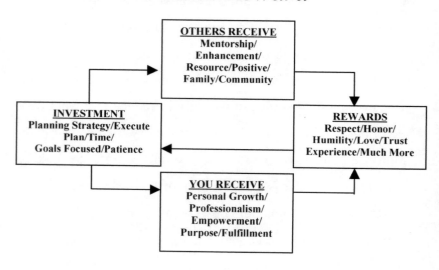

Figure 7: Rewards

Strategize

What is your strategy for reaching your goals and increasing your value? Hopefully, this has become a part of your focus. At this point, you can see from your blueprints that a well thought out plan is very important. The great thing about having the blueprints that you started in the previous chapters is that they have become permanent documentation for your reference. If you have not begun your blueprints, please review the previous chapters before moving on to the next one. The important thing about strategizing is to plan carefully and remember that if you want to acquire a certain lifestyle or social status, you need to start preparing now. When you have a future target in sight, line yourself up to move in that direction.

Nothing's in your way

There may be obstacles that will try to stop you or slow you down. These obstacles could be the environment, stale thinking, lack of information, or lack of inspiration. Whatever the case may be, it can lead to sure failure if not addressed. Just press forward with energy and courage.

By now, you have discovered that any obstacle you face can be overcome. In fact, the only obstacle that is insurmountable is the one that you refuse to go around or jump over. You can do it. There are many people who have done it before you. If obstacles occur, take some time to rest your mind. Haven't you heard the saying – tomorrow is a new day. In other words, sometimes a good overnight rest is all the mind needs to regenerate. The solution will come to you when your mind is well rested.

Obstacles are problems, and problems can be worked out. In fact, the obstacles you face may be the same ones that others around you are facing. So don't be selfish; when you work out your problem, write it down on the following Finding Solutions Chart and determine how many other people your solution can help. It just might be useful to others. Inventors and thinkers do this everyday. It helps you to become a problem solver.

Blueprint 6

Finding Solutions Chart		
WHAT IS THE PROBLEM?	WHO DOES IT AFFECT?	HOW DID IT AFFECT YOU?
WHAT IS A POSITIVE OUTLOOK?	WHAT IS THE SOLUTION?	HOW MANY PEOPLE CAN IT HELP?

Table 10: Solutions

Nearing the finish line

I thought long and hard about how to end this book, and eventually decided to leave you with a few last words of encouragement. Before my final decision, I thought about embedding documentation from other specialists or works from famous psychologists. There are a lot of different works out there. I'm sure psychologists have thoroughly explored the subjects that I have written about. You can look them up and read about them for yourself.

However, many people don't need a psychologist. They have been stuck in the rut because of a lazy mindset or the tendency to blame others for their problems and failures -- instead of taking responsibility for their own lives. The fact is that the blame game is most destructive to the person who is doing the blaming. It causes people to lose focus of the real issues. What I'm saying is that regardless if people have hurt you in the past or have done things to intentionally hold you back from obtaining goals, now is the time to escape from the perils of the blame game and move forward with your life.

If you are angry with someone, more than likely you have internalized this feeling, and the person you are angry with doesn't feel half the grief you are feeling. So, if you think you are hurting them, remember that it's only a thought. Incidentally, if this has been your case for a long period of time, just think about how it is affecting you. Don't fool yourself any longer by saying you're okay. Sometimes it may feel good to blame others, but in the end, who is it really hurting? Break free of this worthless activity, stop blaming others and move forward.

The bottom line is that at the end of the day, there will be no one but you starring back from the mirror. If you don't invest in yourself, no one else will either. Today, blueprint your future and set higher goals for your life. There will be challenges as you set out on your journey. It won't always be easy. In fact, it will sometimes be tedious and tiring. But just remember that it is a journey. It is one that is full of your dreams, your hopes, followed by intentions, commitment, patience, and enduring the good and the bad. Therefore, I encourage you to move forward.

My goal is to touch you in a positive way with this material. I thank you for going on this journey with me. If I have encouraged you in any way, it is truly an honor. If I have caused you to rethink your past or readjust your schedule to find time for planning a better future, or if you have learned one good or new thing from this book, then I am truly satisfied with the message. So, go ahead and finish your personal blueprint. Your future depends on what you do now. May your blueprint have a strong foundation, so you can build a satisfying life and keep moving forward.

There may be times when you will feel you are not making progress, but if you continue to follow your plans, you will begin to see your goals materialize. They will come closer and closer until one day you will be able to reach out and literally live them. You will have overcome the obstacles, ironed out problems, and learned from mistakes. You will have gotten that certificate, diploma or degree, mastered that project, or started that business. I encourage you to stay focused, committed, and to keep moving forward.

Do you remember the famous tale of the race between the tortoise and the hare? Well, also remember this. The race isn't always given to the fast, and neither to the powerful, but to him that endures the race. Endure! It may take a little longer than you anticipated, but stay with it. It may be a lot harder than you thought it would be, but the pain only lasts for a season, a semester, or a day. Believe me, the rewards will last much longer and satisfy you with a lifetime of achievements. Just keep moving forward.

Positive Proclamations

The list of proclamations below is only the beginning of the list to help you begin your own list of proclamations. Incorporate positive words and statements into your vocabulary and your life. Create a positive environment for yourself, and you will attract the positive. When making life decisions, it is good to have a positive attitude. If there are times when you can't think of good things to say to yourself or others, just refer to your list and choose something great. This will help you avoid negative thinking and speaking. It's nice when others give you a pat on the back, but when you believe in yourself, it is the greatest gift that you can give yourself.

Proclamations for Success

1) *My greatness lies within my inner being.*

2) *I am successful.*

3) *I will go after what I want in life.*

4) *I am a positive and powerful thinker.*

5) *I will share my greatness with the world.*

6) *I will use my potential to the fullest.*

_____

_____

_____

_____

_____

_____

_____

_____

_____

_____

Principle 6:
Commitment and endurance is the key to obtaining success.

✓ Plan, Strategize and Execute.

✓ Integrate into positive environments.

✓ Have plans that make a positive impact.

✓ Believing in yourself is the greatest gift you can have.

✓ Become a problem solver.

The race isn't always given to the fastest, and neither to the strongest, but to him that endures to the end. Endure.

Blueprint Notes 6

Name some of the things in which you are planning to dedicate more time and commitment.

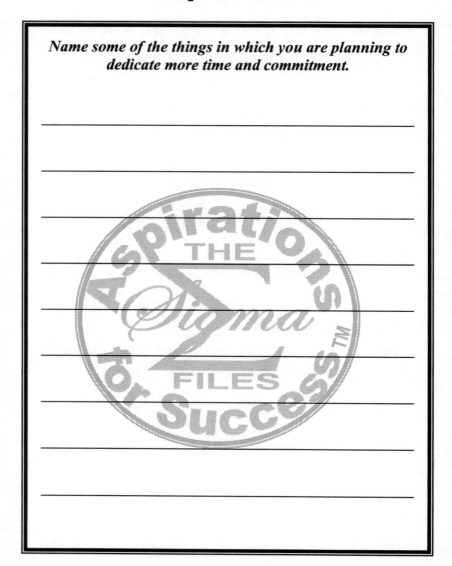

_____

_____

_____

_____

_____

_____

_____

Celebrate Chapter 6

Celebrate your legacy!

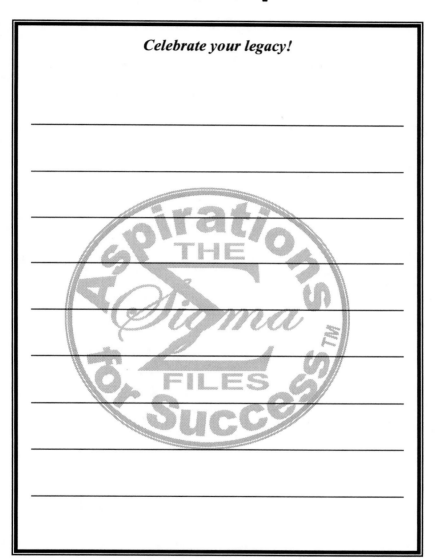

Advantages to blueprinting your future and disadvantages to not blueprinting your future

ADVANTAGES	DISADVANTAGES
Benefactor	Behind
Liberating	Lost
Upper Hand	Unbalanced
Empowering	Empty
Possibilities	Plight
Respectability	Regretful
Intelligence	Ignorance
Nobility	Nonsense
Transforming	Trampled
Initiative	Inferior
Nascent	Nothing
Growth	Gaffe

Notes

Notes

Notes

Notes

Notes

Certificate of Completion

Awarded to

_____

for successfully completing

On this date: _____

Signed: _Linda J. Loving_
Author

Products or Services

ASPIRATIONS FOR SUCCESS Book - Inspires you to anticipate your future, plan your future, and be encouraged about your plans. **Price: $12.95** **Item #: 0001** **Type: Paperback**	**PRODUCT OR SERVICE** Describe the product or service here. Include a brief description and any features. **Price: $00.00** **Item #: 000000** **Type: Type**
EXTRA WORKBOOK Forms from *Aspirations for Success* book. **Price: $10.95** **Item #: 000002** **Type: 8x10 Grayscale**	**PRODUCT OR SERVICE** Describe the product or service here. Include a brief description and any features. **Price: $00.00** **Item #: 000000** **Type: Type**
T-SHIRT - ASPIRATIONS FOR SUCCESS: THE SIGMA FILE™ The Sigma File logo. **Price: $16.00 S, M, L, XL** **Price: $17.50 XXL, XXXL** **Item #: 0003** **Type: White Cotton**	**PRODUCT OR SERVICE** Describe the product or service here. Include a brief description and any features. **Price: $00.00** **Item #: 000000** **Type: Type**
PRODUCT OR SERVICE Describe the product or service here. Include a brief description and any features. **Price: $00.00** **Item #: 000000** **Type: Type**	**PRODUCT OR SERVICE** Describe the product or service here. Include a brief description and any features. **Price: $00.00** **Item #: 000000** **Type: Type**

ACME Training Order Form

Last Name					
First Name				M.I.	
Address				Apt./Unit	
City		State	ZIP Code		
Phone	( )	E-Mail:			

Method of payment	☐	☐	
	Check	Money Order	

Made payable to: ACME Training

Please allow 4 to 6 weeks for delivery.

Item No.	Price	Qty.	Amount
	Subtotal		
	Tax		
	Shipping		

Shipping is additional: $4.95 for the 1st item, $1.00 each additional item up to 24 items. $24.95 on 25 items or more. For corporate shipping check website. Purchases must be paid by checks, or money order. Please do not send cash through the mail.

ACME Training, P.O. Box 320146, Flint, MI 48532
Website: www.acmetraining.net
Email: afs@acmetraining.net
(ACME: *Aspiration, Confidence, Motivation and Education*)

INDEX TABLE

Name Reference
Leontyne Price
Jesse Norman
Barbara Streisand

Reference Quotes
Maya Angelou
Walt Disney
Colin Powell
Oprah Winfrey
Albert Einstein

Book Reference
T. Harv Eker. Secrets of the Millionaire Mind. New York:
Harper Business, 2005, pages 112-114.

The Merriam –Webster Dictionary

About the Author

Linda J. Loving has experience spanning education and business. She earned a Bachelor's of Business Administration degree with a concentration in Organizational Behavior and Human Resources from The University of Michigan-Flint. She is currently employed in the Human Resources and is pursuing a Master of Science Administration degree. Mrs. Loving started ACME Training in 2008 in order to share her passion for providing inspiration to help others who desire to succeed at accomplishing their goals.

Mission Statement

ACME Training's mission is empower people by building a network of resources and delivering educational and inspirational products and services to individuals, to communities, and to the world.

ASPIRATIONS FOR SUCCESS

Blueprinting Your Future

It's not enough to only state there is a need in a certain area of society for mentoring and motivating or to only talk about helping people set goals for their future as if they themselves are not listening. In this book, you will find interaction and assessments to help solve issues that may have stopped, slowed, or caused you to take a detour from your personal goal setting

Linda J. Loving, Author

plans. Don't just sit quietly as others attain their goals. Draw up your own plan to succeed, and put your plan into action with Aspirations for Success, Blueprinting Your Future.

"To have an aspiration is to have a strong desire to achieve something noble. Many of us have aspirations, but don't quite know what to do with them. That is why I have laid out six basic principles in this book, wherein you can begin to create a self study that will lead you in the right direction to becoming successful."

What will you learn?

- Chapter 1: Who Are You? - Knowing ones self.
- Chapter 2: Inner Being – Your inner characteristics.
- Chapter 3: Outer Action – Your inner self influences your outer actions.
- Chapter 4: The Mentor – Encourages you to network.
- Chapter 5: Get in the Competition – Get into the game.
- Chapter 6: The building of a legacy empowers you to reach for goals that return great rewards.